On the Brink of the Abyss

Alain de Benoist

On the Brink of the Abyss

The Imminent Bankruptcy of the Financial System

LONDON
ARKTOS
2015

Copyright © 2015 by Arktos Media Ltd.

All rights reserved. No part of this book may be reproduced or utilised in any form or by any means (whether electronic or mechanical), including photocopying, recording or by any information storage and retrieval system, without permission in writing from the publisher.

Printed in the United Kingdom.

First English edition published in 2015 by Arktos Media Ltd., originally published as *Au bord du gouffre: la faillite annoncée du système de l'argent* (Paris: Krisis, 2011).

ISBN 978-1-910524-30-5

BIC-CLASSIFICATION
Economic and financial crises and disasters (KCX)
Political science and theory (JPA)

TRANSLATOR
Alexander Jacob

EDITORS
John B Morgan and Matthew Peters

COVER DESIGN
Andreas Nilsson

LAYOUT
Tor Westman

ARKTOS MEDIA LTD
www.arktos.com

CONTENTS

Foreword: Money 7

The Origins of the Financial Crisis 11

The Dollar, at the Heart of the Crisis 26

Free Trade and Protectionism 36

Death on Credit 56

Public Debt: How States Have Become Prisoners of Banks 61

The Euro Should Be Made a Common Currency 80

Middle Classes and Working Classes: A Politics of Poverty 87

Immigration, the Reserve Army of Capital 116

Should a Citizenship Income Be Instituted? 124

Afterword: Confronting the Capitalist System 149

Index 186

To Pierre Le Vigan

Foreword: Money

Of course, everybody prefers to have a little more money than a little less. 'Money does not equal happiness, but contributes to it,' goes the popular adage. But it would still be necessary to know what happiness is. Max Weber[1] wrote in 1905, 'A man does not "by nature" wish to earn more and more money, but simply to live as he is accustomed to live and to earn as much as is necessary for that purpose.'[2] Since then, numerous studies have shown that there is only a weak correlation between the rise in the standard of living and the degree of individual satisfaction: beyond a certain threshold, having more does not make one happier. In 1974, Richard Easterlin[3] demonstrated that the average level of satisfaction declared by world populations had remained practically unchanged since 1945, despite a spectacular wealth increase in developed countries. (This phenomenon, known as the 'Easterlin Paradox,' has recently been reconfirmed.) The inability of the indices measuring material growth, like the gross domestic product (GDP), to evaluate actual well-being is also well known — above all at the collective level, since there is no indisputably held rule that allows individual preferences to be aggregated into social preferences.

---

1   Max Weber (1864–1920) was a German who is considered one of the founders of sociology. His principal work is *The Protestant Ethic and the Spirit of Capitalism*.—Ed.

2   Max Weber, *The Protestant Ethic and the Spirit of Capitalism*, trans. Talcott Parsons (Mineola, NY: Dover Publications, 2003), p. 60.—Ed.

3   Richard Easterlin (b. 1926) is a Professor of Economics at the University of Southern California. Benoist is referring to his essay, 'Does Economic Growth Improve the Human Lot? Some Empirical Evidence,' in *Nations and Households in Economic Growth: Essays in Honor of Moses Abramovitz*, ed. Paul A. David and Melvin W. Reder (New York: Academic Press, 1974), pp. 89–125.—Ed.

It is tempting to see in money only an instrument of power. The old project of radically dissociating power from wealth (either one is rich or powerful) will, unfortunately, remain a dream for a long time yet. Once, one was rich because one was powerful; today, one is powerful because one is rich. The accumulation of money has quickly become not a means for commercial expansion, as some consider it, but the very goal of the production of goods. The capitalist system's only aim is the indefinite increase of profits and the endless accumulation of money. The ability to accumulate money clearly gives an arbitrary power to those who possess it. Many governments are at the mercy of financial speculators. And speculative robbery remains capitalism's preferred method of acquisition.

Money should not, however, be confused with currency. The birth of currency can be explained by the development of commercial exchange. In fact, it is only in exchange that objects acquire an economic dimension. Only then can the economic value of items be objectively determined, since the perceived value of goods involved in an exchange can be measured in relation to one another. Being a generally accepted measure of value, currency is intrinsically unifying. By reducing all goods to a common denominator, it renders exchanges homogeneous. Aristotle already noted, 'This is why all things that are exchanged must be somehow comparable. It is for this end that money has been introduced, and it becomes in a sense an intermediary for it measures all things.'[4] By creating a perspective from which the value of even the most unlike things can be expressed by a number, currency renders them, in a way, equal: it reduces all the qualities that set them apart to a simple logic of more or less. Money is that universal standard which allows us to ensure the abstract equivalence of all merchandise. It is the general equivalent which forces all qualities to be expressed in terms of quantity, since the market is capable only of a quantitative differentiation.

---

[4] Aristotle, *Nicomachean Ethics*, Chapter 5, in *The Basic Works of Aristotle* (New York: Random House, 1941), p. 1011.—Ed.

At the same time, exchange also equalises the personality of the participants in the trade. By revealing the compatibility of their supply and their demand, it establishes the interchangeability of their desires and, eventually, the interchangeability of the men who are the locus of these desires. 'The reign of money,' observes Jean-Joseph Goux, 'is the reign of the *only* measure according to which all human things and activities can be evaluated ... A certain monotheistic configuration of the *general equivalent* value form clearly appears here. Monetary rationality, based on a single standard of measurement of values, is an integral part of a certain theological monotheism.' It is the monotheism of the market. 'Money,' writes Marx, 'is the absolutely alienable commodity, because it is all other commodities divested of their shape, the product of their universal alienation.'[5]

Money is thus much more than money — and the greatest mistake would be to believe that it is 'neutral'. Money, no more than science, technology, or language, is not neutral. Twenty-three centuries ago, Aristotle already observed that 'the avarice of mankind is insatiable'.[6] Insatiable is the word, as there is never enough money — and because there is never enough, there can never be too much. The desire for money is a desire that can never be satisfied because it feeds upon itself. Every quantity, whatever it may be, can always be augmented by one more unit. The *best* therefore becomes synonymous with the *most*. That of which one can always have *more*, one never has *enough* of. It is indeed for this reason that the ancient European religions continually warned against the passion for money: the myth of Gullveig,[7] the myth of Midas, the myth of the ring of Polycrates[8] — the

---

5   Karl Marx, from *Capital*, in *Selected Writings* (Indianapolis: Hackett, 1994), p. 252.—Ed.

6   Aristotle, *The Politics*, Book II, in *The Politics, and Constitution of Athens* (Cambridge: Cambridge University Press, 1996), p. 45.—Ed.

7   Gullveig was a sorceress who was obsessed with gold. When she gained an audience with the Aesir (the Nordic gods), she talked about nothing else, angering the gods, who in turn destroyed her.—Ed.

8   Polycrates was a tyrant of Samos during the sixth century BCE. According to Herodotus, he was advised by the Egyptian Pharaoh to throw away that which he valued most in order to avoid bad luck. Polycrates possessed a ring which he valued dearly, and threw it into the sea. However, a fish was later caught that was brought to Polycrates' kitchen that was found to have the ring in its stomach. This caused the Egyptians to break their alliance with him, believing him to be doomed, and Polycrates was later assassinated.—Ed.

'twilight of the gods' (*Ragnarök*) itself being the result of greed (the 'gold of the Rhine').

'We run the risk,' wrote Michel Winock some years ago, 'of seeing money and financial success become the only standard for social consideration and the only goal of life.' It is precisely this point that we have reached. Nowadays, money produces unanimity. The political Right has long ago become its servant. The institutional Left, under the pretext of 'realism', has rallied loudly behind the market economy and the liberal management of capital. The language of economics has become omnipresent. Money is henceforth the obligatory conduit of all the forms of desire that are experienced within the range of the market. The financial system, however, has only so much time left. Money will perish by money, that is, by hyperinflation, mass bankruptcies, and excessive indebtedness. Then, perhaps, people will understand that one is never truly rich except in that which one has given to others.

The Origins of the Financial Crisis

It is often said that capitalism is synonymous with crisis, that it feeds on the crises that it provokes, and even that its ability to adapt is unlimited, thus letting us understand that it is indestructible. In reality, one must distinguish between short-term, cyclical crises and structural, systemic crises (such as those which occurred between 1870 and 1893, then during the Great Depression of 1929–1930, and again between 1973 and 1982, when structural unemployment began to appear in Western countries).

The economic cycles that have been described by economists like Nikolai Kondratiev[9] or Joseph Schumpeter[10] can be classified within what the historian Fernand Braudel[11] called the time of 'long duration'. The cycles highlighted by Kondratiev in 1926 encompass 40 to 60 years and are divided into two phases. In phase A — the rising phase — profits are fundamentally generated by production. In phase B — the declining phase — capitalism, in order to continue to increase profits, gradually turns to financialisation. Capital is increasingly diverted from production to speculation, ceasing to provide opportunities for work by means of productive investments.

---

9 Nikolai Kondratiev (1892–1938) was a Russian economist who became one of the primary advocates of Lenin's New Economic Policy in the 1920s. He later postulated the existence of what came to be termed Kondratiev waves, which he said were long-term cycles of boom and bust in the global capitalist economy over the course of four to six decades. He was executed during Stalin's Great Purge.—Ed.

10 Joseph Schumpeter (1883–1950) was an Austrian economist who later emigrated to the United States. He developed the idea of business cycles, consisting of a series of fluctuations in the global economy over periods from a few years to several decades.—Ed.

11 Fernand Braudel (1902–1985) was a French historian who used the term 'long duration' to describe the long-term effects of material and geographical factors on the development of civilisations.—Ed.

Phase A, characterised by the invention and diffusion of numerous innovations, is progressively accompanied by an excess of investments made in order to meet increasing competition, which provokes a rise in prices and interest rates and is the prelude to the next phase of the cycle. In the descending phase, B, massive debts are incurred both by states and households. Along with the over-accumulation of capital, financial power becomes the *sine qua non* of all strategies aimed at increasing profitability. In the final stage, the speculative 'bubbles' burst one after the other, unemployment increases, bankruptcies multiply, and so on. In this climate of general destruction of value (falling stock prices, businesses shutting down, and unprofitable sectors being liquidated), the economy finds itself in a state of deflation. The system then becomes chaotic and increasingly intolerable, with political and social troubles arising to aggravate the situation.

Many economists believe that today we are in phase B of a cycle initiated approximately 35 years ago, and that the international financial crisis which began in the United States in the autumn of 2008 is, indeed, a structural crisis corresponding to a rupture of the dynamic coherence of the entire system. Coming after the petrol crises of 1973 and 1979, the debt crisis of developing countries in 1982, the crash of the stock markets and rising interest rates of 1987, the American recession of 1991, the Asian crisis of 1997, and the burst of the dot-com bubble in 2001, this crisis, much stronger than the preceding ones, is unquestionably the most serious there has been since the 1930s, all the more now that it is unfolding in a world that has become globalised.

However, trying to explain this crisis using cycles has only a limited value. It tends to make one think that these crises fall within the normal framework of capitalism: there are always highs and lows, and that this is the nature of the system. There is no real reason to be worried. But now, we are in fact confronted with a triple crisis of a new sort: a crisis of the capitalist system, a crisis of liberal globalisation, and a crisis of American hegemony.

The explanation most often advanced to interpret the origins of the present crisis is the debt incurred by American households in the form of real estate mortgage loans (the infamous 'subprimes'). This is not untrue, but it is seldom asked why they are in debt.

The eternal problem of capitalism is that of markets. Originally, capitalism sought to sell increasingly more to people whom it tended to increasingly deprive of purchasing power. On the one side, it congratulated itself when it saw its profits increasing to the detriment of the incomes derived from work, while on the other it saw clearly that, in the final analysis, it was necessary that consumption should increase in order that profits could continue to rise. Lowering salaries also reduces consumption. In the Fordist phase of capitalism it was realised that it served no purpose to endlessly increase production if people lacked the means to consume what was being produced. Salaries were therefore progressively increased with the sole purpose of supporting consumption. This phase, which is now coming to its end, saw its apogee in the period of the 'Thirty Glorious Years'. In what Frédéric Lordon calls 'the capitalism of low-pressure wages', the Fordist logic of increasing salaries in order to feed and sustain consumption is now being abandoned. In its place we see a return to the initial form of capitalism where the distribution of revenues between capital and the wage-earners was seen as a zero-sum game: everything won by one side is lost by the other.

How can more money be made in an economic climate where profit margins tend to shrink? One solution is to hire cheap, unqualified workers who do not complain. This explains why employers have always favoured immigration. They consider immigrants to be a reserve army of capital, enabling them to depress the salaries of the local workforce.

The third solution, which is the one to which capitalism has had major recourse since the Second World War, and above all since the 1980s, is credit. By means of credit, Western countries have chosen to privilege consumption as a motor of growth instead of investment or exports. If people go into debt, they have more money to spend and can consume more. The problem with this scheme of supporting consumption through credit is that the consumers must sooner or later pay back their debts — something they are unable to do when incomes stagnate or diminish. On the other hand, 'a great abyss opens between the demands of a consumption frenetically stimulated by credit and the capacity of the economy to respond to it, hence the appeal to other countries, resulting in a chronic commercial deficit and provoking massive debt' (Yves-Marie Laulan). This was one of the major components of the crisis of autumn 2008. In the United States, where consumption has reached the extraordinary ratio of 73% of the GDP, while the savings rate is almost non-existent, the average rate of household debt (the ratio of their total debt in relation to their disposable income) was, in 2008, around 120%. The household debt rate has also exploded in the majority of other Western countries, in addition to excessive public and corporate debt. The situation is explosive.

Salaries are today crushed between being restricted by shareholders on one hand and competition on the other.

One of the dominant features of 'turbo-capitalism',[12] corresponding to the third wave of the history of capitalism, is the complete domination of financial markets. This domination increases the power of capital owners. Desirous of obtaining ever higher and quicker returns on their investments, the shareholders force down salaries and opportunistically outsource production to emerging countries where the rise of productivity goes hand-in-hand with very low wages. At the same time, businesses try to achieve better rates of productivity by laying off workers. The surplus value generated by businesses becoming the spoils of capital more than the revenues of labour, salary deflation results in the stagnation or reduction of purchasing power, and the diminution of global solvent demand. Competition, for its part, is expressed in new terms in the epoch of globalisation. One example

---

12 The term 'turbo-capitalism' was coined by Edward Luttwak in his book *Turbo-Capitalism: Winners and Losers in the Global Economy* (New York: HarperCollins, 1999), which he saw as a form of accelerated capitalism lacking restraints or any sense of balance.—Ed.

is the increased use of outsourcing, which places the wage-earners of developed countries in competition with workers on the other side of the globe who perform the same work, often under atrocious conditions, at absolute *dumping* rates.[13]

The final result is that salaries become a variable of macro-economic adjustment and job losses multiply. The present strategy of capital owners is to reduce salaries while aggravating the precariousness of the labour market, thus producing a relative impoverishment of the working and middle classes who, in the hope of maintaining their standard of living, see no other option than to go deeper into debt even though their ability to repay their debts grows steadily worse.

The option for households to borrow in order to cover their current expenses or to acquire a house has been the major financial innovation of post-war capitalism. The economies were then stimulated by an artificial demand based on credit facilities. Across the Atlantic, this tendency has been encouraged since the 1990s by the granting of increasingly favourable credit conditions without any consideration of the solvency of the borrowers. In this way, an attempt was made to compensate for the decrease of solvent demand that had resulted from the reduction of salaries. In other words, consumption was stimulated through credit, for want of being able to stimulate it by increasing purchasing power. That was the only way for capital owners to find new opportunities for profit, albeit at the price of risks that were not taken into account.

This is the origin of the staggering debt of American households, who have, for a long time, chosen to consume rather than to save (American households are today twice as indebted as French households and three times as indebted as Italian households). Next, people speculated on these 'rotten debts' by means of 'securitisation'. This allowed big actors in the credit industry to free themselves from the risk of borrowers becoming

---

13 Dumping refers to the practice of manufacturers who export goods to another country at a cost that is lower than the price it commands in its home market.—Ed.

insolvent by selling their debts. 'Securitisation', which is one of the major financial innovations of post-war capitalism, consists in consolidating loans given by a bank or a credit company into a financial instrument that is then sold (including the credit risk) to other investors in the financial markets. In this way, a vast credit market has been created, which is also a market where risk is bought and sold. This market collapsed in 2008. The acceleration of the credit mechanisms which technically sparked off the crisis in the United States thus results from the attempt of capital to maintain the capacity for consumption of as many people as possible, while simultaneously depressing wages. The present crisis started when credit evaporated. The extraordinary megalomania and greed of the executive officers of the big companies and the big commercial or investment banks did the rest.

We are also witnessing a crisis of liberal globalisation, however. The brutal effect of the American mortgage crisis on markets all over the world is the direct consequence of a globalisation conceived and realised by financial interests. Beyond its immediate cause, it constitutes the culmination of 40 years of deregulation in accordance with a globalised economic model based on liberal recipes. It is, in fact, the ideology of deregulation that led to the American debt crisis, just as it was the root cause of the Mexican (1995), Asian (1997), Russian (1998), and Argentinean (2001) crises. Globalisation, at the same time that it made many types of outsourcing possible, has reinforced the concentric orientation of world financial markets around the American pole. It also permits capital to circulate freely across the world without any oversight. It thus gives to the financial markets, which are themselves globalised and completely deterritorialised, a dominant position, which reinforces the financialisation of capital in relation to the real economy. With currency no longer being issued in proportion to created wealth (the sum of goods and services produced), immense, virtual financial masses move at an increasing speed around the globe in search of profitable investments. Globalisation has created a situation in which major crises in one part of the world spread almost instantaneously, in a 'viral' manner, as the sociologist Jean Baudrillard[14] would have said, over the entire planet. That is why the American crisis so quickly affected the European financial markets, beginning with the credit markets, with all the consequences that such a shock wave could have at a time when the European economy, like that of America, was already on the verge of a recession.

Finally, one should not lose sight of the fact that this international crisis began in the United States — a country that has to deal with an abysmal budget deficit, growing public debt, and colossal trade deficits. For ten years, the motor of economic growth in America has not been real production, but rather the expansion of debt and the monetary advantage resulting from the international dominance of the dollar.

The fact that the dollar is at the same time a national currency and the world's reserve currency of choice, and has been free from all connection with gold since 1971,[15] has for a long time allowed the United States to affirm its hegemony and make it felt even while continuing to register colossal deficits. This has been done at the expense of Americans indebting themselves to countries with positive trade balances. In the future, the anxiety of the large public and private funds which, notably in Asia, hold considerable quantities of American public and semi-public instruments (such as treasury bonds), and thus so many debts incurred by the United States, will be determinative. At present, 70% of all the foreign reserves in the world are held in American dollars, a proportion that bears no relation to the actual size of the American economy. In the years to come, it is possible that oil-exporting countries may slowly abandon the dollar (the famous 'petrodollars') for the euro. In the long term, such a situation could end in countries like China and Russia grouping together to conceive an alternative project to the present international financial order. George Soros said

---

14 Jean Baudrillard (1929–2007) was a French sociologist and cultural theorist who is regarded as one of the most important postmodernist thinkers.—Ed.

15 President Richard Nixon took the US dollar off the gold standard in 1971.—Ed.

it plainly in January 2008: 'The world is rushing towards the end of the era of the dollar.'[16]

We hear frequent assurances that increased regulation or 'making the system moral' would be enough to avoid these sorts of crises. Politicians are happy to speak of 'corruption in the financial markets', while others stigmatise the 'irresponsibility' of the bankers, attempting to show us that the crisis is due only to inadequate regulation, and that a return to more 'transparent' practices would allow the return of a less carnivorous capitalism. This is a double error, first, because it is precisely the impotence of the politicians to face the problems inherent in deregulated financial markets that has opened the way for the total liberalisation of the financial system. Second, and above all, because this is to ignore the fact that the very nature of capitalism makes it a system alien to every moral consideration. 'Capital resents every limit as a fetter,' said Karl Marx. The logic of the accumulation of capital is lack of limitation, the rejection of every limit, the rule of the world by the logic of the market and the transformation of all values into goods, the *Ge-stell* of which Heidegger spoke.[17]

In the phases of the over-accumulation of capital, the reinforcement of financial power becomes the lever determining every strategy which aims at increasing the profitability of capital. But, beyond finance alone, it is in fact the domination of the entire economy by the sole criterion of profitability, without consideration of the human factors, of the lost jobs, of the ruined lives, of the exhaustion of natural resources, and of the non-commercial costs (so-called 'negative externalities'), that is called into question by the financial crisis. The root cause of this crisis is the ambition to achieve the largest possible financial profit in the shortest time possible, to the exclusion of every other consideration.

---

16 Soros said this at the World Economic Forum in Davos, Switzerland—Ed.

17 Martin Heidegger used the term *Ge-stell*, or 'framing,' to refer to technology as being not a tool, but rather the condition of human life today. He discusses this in *The Question Concerning Technology and Other Essays*, trans. William Lovitt (New York: Harper & Row, 1977).—Ed.

What is going to happen now? Since the United States bailed out the banks to prevent their collapse, the problem of private debt has aggravated the problem of public debt. Can the crisis eventually bring about, through a domino effect, a chain of payment defaults by all parties involved, and thus a collapse of the entire international financial system? Things have not yet gone so far. But, in the best of cases, the economic crisis is going to continue for a long while, with a widespread recession which will cause a rise in unemployment. Profits will shrink, which will inevitably have repercussions on the financial markets. Contrary to what certain people wish, the fortunes of the speculative economy directly affects the real economy. Businesses depend on the banking system, even if it is only for the credit that they need for their investments. The crisis has caused banks, debilitated by the accumulation of bad debts, to drastically cut back on the credit they will grant (the so-called 'credit crunch').

If one manages to temporarily stabilise the system, the shareholders' demand for a return on their investments and the companies' need to remain competitive will continue to push salaries downwards, and one will soon witness new and even larger excesses of debt, which will culminate in a new crisis of an even greater magnitude. Alternatively, if attempts are made to keep household debts under control, consumption will decrease and growth will slow, which would represent an intolerable prospect for capital. In the past, wars offered a possibility to get out of this sort of situation (in the case of the Second World War it was not, as is often maintained, the New Deal which saved the US from the Depression and mass unemployment, but the war which transformed that country into an arms and munitions factory of the Allied powers). Will America resort to such a strategy again, in order to retain its international supremacy?

The United States, which has been living on credit for a long time, had, by 2008, accumulated a public debt exceeding 11,000 billion dollars, that is, about 36,000 dollars per citizen. In addition to that, there was also 50,000 billion dollars in private debts (households and businesses).

In total, each American citizen was indebted in the amount of more than 200,000 dollars! The growth of debts has led to a corresponding increase in the money supply, even though the country where this money is created is in recession, produces less wealth, and goes deeper into debt every day. The actual rate of unemployment has already exceeded 10%, and one already knows that, despite reforms undertaken by President Obama, the number of citizens deprived of any unemployment insurance will soon reach 100 million people, or one in three Americans. In this country, where a recovery would simultaneously demand a lowering of consumption, an increase in private savings, and a reduction of deficits, the banking system has, in reality, already become insolvent.

The present crisis is often compared to that of 1929. It is, in reality, more serious for at least three reasons. On the one hand, this is the first true international financial crisis (the crisis of 1929, often represented as such, was in fact limited to the United States and Europe), its scope reflecting the realities of globalisation, which emerged after the collapse of the Soviet system. On the other hand, companies depend much more on the banking system than before; since the 1980s easily available credit has been the key to the growth of the gross national product. Finally, the United States, which was still a rising power in 1929, is today on the decline, and is also the epicentre of the crisis.

The collapse of the Soviet system resulted from a systemic crisis. Could it also happen to the capitalist system? Some think so, as, for example, the economist Immanuel Wallerstein.[18] According to him we have 'in the last thirty years entered into the final phase of the capitalist system', for capitalism does not manage to 'constitute a system' any longer, being unable to regain its equilibrium after having deviated too much from its stable posi-

---

18 Immanuel Wallerstein (b. 1930) is an American sociologist who has long opposed both liberalism and globalisation. His ideas are centred upon the concept of the 'World System'. Wallerstein denies that there is a distinction between the First World and the Third World, and holds that the entire globe has been subject to a single, global capitalist system since the nineteenth century. This World System has brought about the commodification of all aspects of human life and has caused inequalities to grow between nations and classes.—Ed.

tion. Wallerstein goes so far as to evoke a transition period comparable to that which saw European civilisation move from the feudal system to the capitalist system.

Now, despite the proclamations of the G20, world leaders persist in acting as if the international financial system was only a victim of a crisis of growth, of a passing disturbance, which could be remedied by the establishment of 'international financial governance' effected through certain measures of 'regulation', massive injections of new liquidity, granting new means to the International Monetary Fund (IMF), lower interest rates, plans for the repurchase of 'toxic bank assets' and 'rotten speculative products' (which only shift the cost of exiting the crisis from privately-held corporations to states), plans for the revival of industries threatened by bankruptcy, a superficial questioning of 'tax havens', and so on. The way in which these leaders have unanimously condemned protectionism and affirmed that globalisation should be continued at any cost shows that they have not at all taken into consideration the systemic and historic character of this crisis, which also characterises the bankruptcy of the project of the so-called 'New World Order' formulated in the 1990s. Moreover, these measures are doomed to fail, since many countries have large deficits and must, in order to service their debts, find surpluses which they are unable to obtain unless they do so by draconian budget cuts that are likely to plunge them into deep and lasting recession, at a point in time when their export capacities have been reduced by their loss of competitiveness. In reality, there is every reason to think that the hundreds of billions of dollars or euros created *ex nihilo*[19] by the central banks will only generate new 'bubbles', even more monstrously noxious than the preceding ones. The risk is very great that such measures will create hyperinflation rather than economic growth. Hyperinflation may wipe out debts, but may also, in a climate of widespread depression, end in numerous bankruptcies, in a global explosion of unemployment, in the sudden collapse of all pension systems and,

---

19   Latin: 'out of nothing'.—Ed.

when the United States is compelled to monetise its colossal national debt, which other nations are unlikely to finance in the long run, in the definitive collapse of the dollar.

Ultimately, the crisis that we are experiencing today is not only a financial and banking crisis, nor even simply an economic crisis. It is a systemic crisis of the regime of endless accumulation that is characteristic of the present phase of capitalism, which also marks the culmination of what one could call, from a philosophical or historical point of view, the dialectic of credit.

* * *

There are at least three lessons to be drawn from this international financial crisis, which is evidently far from over. The first, and the most immediately apparent, is a flagrant denial of the liberal thesis, presented at length by Mandeville in his *Fable of the Bees*,[20] according to which private vices are synonymous with public virtue: it is claimed that individual, egoistic behaviours contribute to the collective advantage, for, by attempting to maximise their own profits, individuals and corporations increase the total wealth, thereby benefiting all of society. According to this thesis, the interests of the 'merchants' are perfectly consistent with the happiness of all and the greater good. However, the deregulation of some economies since the Reagan-Thatcher years shows, on the contrary, that rapacity set up as a general principle ends, in reality, in the enrichment of a few and in the impoverishment of the many. Economics left entirely to itself, unchecked speculation, the quest for instantaneous capital gain, frenzied accumulation of debt, 'bubbles' bursting one after the other, the accelerated resale of securitised products; all that has only one final result: a 'social and human catastrophe of the greatest magnitude' (Jacques Julliard).

---

20 Bernard Mandeville (1670–1733) was an Anglo-Dutch philosopher. His book, *Fable of the Bees*, outlined his economic thought and anticipated many of the ideas which were later codified by Adam Smith, such as the division of labour.—Ed.

The second lesson relates to the 'invisible hand'[21] which, according to liberal theoreticians, not only permits supply and (solvent) demand to adjust itself miraculously, but also permits capitalism to triumph naturally over its crises, the market system being at once self-regulatory and self-regulated. 'The crisis is the proof that the market regulates itself', somebody went so far as to say recently! The postulate is that of a normative conception of social life based on the primacy of *laissez-faire*[22] and the self-sufficiency of a market considered as a moral authority that is always right. But, as regards self-regulation and the 'invisible hand', it is towards the very visible hand of the state that the big insurance companies and banks threatened with bankruptcy have turned, ever since the crisis erupted. They were suddenly content to benefit from the wealth of the same state whose interventions into economic and financial matters they had earlier claimed could only hurt the 'free play' of competition. The state came to the rescue of those responsible for the crisis by injecting billions of dollars into doomed banks, whose losses were thus 'socialised'. Even after this, some continue to pretend that capitalism solves its periodic crises by itself, indeed that liberalism 'is not the cause of, but the solution to, the crisis of globalised capitalism' (Nicolas Baverez)! The crisis shows, in reality, that the world of finance is incapable of regulating itself, and that its capacity for recovery mostly depends on massive injections of public funds, that is, the prompt intervention of the state; such interventions being in principle (the liberals are the first to remind us) contrary to the spontaneous action of the markets.

Finally, what is striking in the present crisis is that, even though everybody repeats that capitalism is affected by cyclical crises, nobody (or nearly nobody) ever seems capable of predicting one. Economics, however, claims to be a science, and, what is more, a science whose principles, properly ap-

---

21 Adam Smith (1723–1790) was a Scottish economist who is regarded as the father of modern capitalism. In his principal work, *The Wealth of Nations*, he used the term 'invisible hand' to describe the way in which the marketplace regulates itself, since individuals end up benefitting society by pursuing their own personal ambitions, even when they have no altruistic intentions.—Ed.

22 Free from state intervention.—Ed.

plied, would enable us to handle risks in a rational fashion and to achieve permanent linear growth. 'The main object of science', said Henri Bergson, 'is to forecast and measure.'[23] Why, then, do mainstream economists seldom succeed in either predicting crises or in identifying means to remedy them? It is because the theory that man can be reduced to a *Homo oeconomicus*[24] leaves much to be desired, to say the least. Social reality cannot be understood by means of equations, for man is neither a fundamentally rational agent always seeking to maximise his own good, nor merely a producer or a consumer. On account of this fact, it is impossible to isolate a 'pure economic object' distinct from the human and social facts with which it is inevitably intertwined. According to neoclassical liberal economics, man can be reduced to numbers and his actions can be predicted. The present crisis provides proof that this claim of 'transparency' is a mistake. History is, in reality, unpredictable. It abounds as much in necessities as in chances, paradoxes, uncertainties, and risks. The world of universal interconnection, of perfect liquidity permitting a totally 'free' circulation of capital, is only a dream. One cannot escape 'opacity', beginning with the financial markets. The growing mathematisation of economic theory that we have been witnessing in the last twenty years, especially in the field of risk calculation, only appears to be scientific. Mathematical formalisation causes economics to gain in elegance what it loses in realism. It leads especially to the neglect of all the factors that are impossible to quantify, beginning precisely with the notion of risk, which depends, above all, on the *significance* that is given to events.

The immediate causes of the crisis (the pressure of competition brought on by globalisation which has standardised the model of a capitalism based on wage deflation, the allocation of surplus value to the detriment of salaries, the lowering of demand and its artificial stimulation through credit,

---

23 Henri Bergson, *Time and Free Will: An Essay on the Immediate Data of Consciousness*, trans. F. L. Pogson (New York: Cosimo, 2008), p. 230. Bergson (1859–1941) was a French philosopher who was very influential in the early twentieth century.—Ed.

24 Latin: 'economic man'.—Ed.

the rise in power of the financial markets and the increasing demands for return on capital) cannot deceive us. The present crisis is not an accidental occurrence. It is not one crisis among others that already occurred in the history of capitalism, but a systemic crisis of the system of accumulation and over-accumulation, that is, of capitalism itself, or of a capitalism which no longer dominates global society only formally, but indeed in actuality. From this point of view, it serves no purpose to denounce the excesses, the 'deviations', or the dysfunctions of a system which is intrinsically excessive. The capitalist system is doomed to perpetual acceleration, and to always increasing its own imbalances. The eternal problem of capitalism is always to find ever more to sell to men who have ever less. This is the ancient curse of chrematistics,[25] that is to say, of money (*ta chremata*).[26]

The fundamental idea to bear in mind is that a capitalism left entirely to its own devices can only self-destruct. It will be undermined by its internal contradictions, resulting from the principle of limitless accumulation, and thus from its own dynamics. The movement of capital reaches its limit when it can no longer constitute a system; that is to say, when the world it creates no longer corresponds to the world that it desires. Small consolation for those who prefer to believe that it would be better to defeat it by attacking it head-on? Perhaps. But it is a fact that everything that exists dies through what gave it birth. It is the same for all the systems that engender alienation: it is that which gives them life and allows them to perpetuate themselves at a given moment is also that which creates the conditions for their disappearance. The predominant article of faith today is that capitalism will live forever. But the truth is that the demon of credit and the political ideology of profit alone, even if attempts are made to perpetuate their careers, will ultimately not escape their destinies.

---

25 Seeing one's sole purpose as using money to acquire more money.—Ed.
26 From ancient Greek.—Ed.

The Dollar, at the Heart of the Crisis

For a good number of economists, one of the causes of the global systemic crisis which we are now witnessing is due to the collapse of the Bretton Woods system based on the American dollar as the pivot of the international monetary system and, more particularly, to what the Chinese economist Xu Xiaonian called the 'over-issue of currency by the Federal Reserve'. Édouard Husson and Norman Palma, for example, think that the crisis is the direct consequence of the 'exorbitant privilege' that allows the United States to 'buy the goods and services of the world with mere paper'.[27] The fact is, in any case, that the tensions within the international monetary system today constitute a crisis within the crisis, and that a bankruptcy of this system would necessarily implicate the collapse of the dollar.

As everyone knows, the dollar occupies a particular status among currencies. Created in 1785,[28] it constitutes the national currency of the United States and its overseas territories (like Puerto Rico), but it is, at the same time, the principal reserve currency, the currency most utilised in the world for commercial transactions, the principal currency dealt with on the exchange market, the currency used on the most important financial mar-

---

27 Édouard Husson and Norman Palma, *Le capitalisme malade de sa monnaie: Considérations sur l'origine véritable des crises économiques* (Paris: François-Xavier de Guibert, 2009), p. 163. The authors advocate the creation of a new international unit of currency with which they would create a transitional system that would then allow a return to the gold standard.

28 The famous maxim 'In God we trust' appeared in 1864 on the two-cent coin. Since 1955 it has been printed on all American notes.

kets, and, since December 2006, second only to the euro in terms of currency in circulation. Already in 1985, more than 80% of international trade was transacted in dollars. The figure increased to 89% in 2004. In 2007, the dollar amounted to 64% of the reserves of central banks in the world (72% in 2002). One also knows that the majority of countries use dollars to pay for the crude petrol that they buy in producing countries, the two principal petrol stock exchanges of the world, those of London and New York, being equally dominated by American businesses.

In order to understand how this came about, a basic historical reminder is necessary.

Until 1810, the monetary system in use in the Western countries was based on bimetallism, with gold and silver as standards. At that time, England chose monometallism in the form of the gold standard. The majority of countries did the same between 1820 and 1876. The monetary system called the Gold Exchange Standard, based on the gold standard, was then instituted in 1922 by the Genoa Conference before being suspended in 1933 by Franklin D Roosevelt, who wished to devalue the dollar. It was restored in 1944 by the Bretton Woods accords.

The Bretton Woods system was based on two principal pillars: a system of fixed exchange rates between currencies and, above all, the recognition of the dollar as the currency of international reserve, the dollar remaining convertible into gold (at the fixed rate of 35 dollars an ounce of fine gold), but only within the scope of exchanges between central banks. In fact, the institutions set up after 1944 sanctioned the relation between economic and political powers in the aftermath of the Second World War: the new domination of the United States, the only country that became richer during this period, the ruin of Europe, and the political non-existence of Asia.

But on 15 August 1971 a thunderbolt struck: President Richard Nixon decided to make the dollar inconvertible in relation to gold, following the accumulation of American deficits during the 1960s, already increased by the expenses associated with the Vietnam War, which had resulted in very strong pressure on the American currency. This decision took the form of a *diktat* — it was made by the United States without any other country being consulted — and was explained at that time in terms of the fear of the American administration of seeing certain countries demanding the conversion of their surplus dollars into gold.

Marking the end of the Bretton Woods system, the inconvertibility of the dollar and its transformation into a simple paper currency was immediately translated into a series of tensions that ended, in December 1971, in the 'Washington Accords' — also called the 'Smithsonian Agreement' — which foresaw central parities and fluctuation margins between currencies not exceeding 2.25%. It was at that time that the American Secretary of the Treasury, John Connally, uttered his famous remark, 'The dollar is now *our* currency and *your* problem.' However, already in March 1973, the Group of Ten (the European Economic Community, Sweden, the United States, Canada, and Japan) decided to abandon the fixed exchange rates of the diverse currencies in relation to the dollar, which allowed the central banks of other countries to stop maintaining parity of their currency with the dollar. A new system, called 'floating exchange rates', was thus born. It would be formally ratified in January 1976 by the Jamaica Accords.

The imbalances then continued. Already in the 1980s, the dollar began to depreciate tendentially. A very high increase in long-term interest rates occurred; then, in October 1987, came the double crash of the bond markets and the stock markets. The depreciation of the dollar was further accelerated as a result of the mortgage crisis, which unleashed the present crisis. While in 2002 a euro was still worth only 86 cents of the dollar, it reached, on 2 June 2009, the rate of $1.43 — the all-time high of one euro for $1.60 having been reached on 15 July 2008. This relative depreciation of the dollar impacts negatively on European exports, as European products become increasingly costly for Americans: it is estimated that the threshold of vulnerability for the European industries is situated around one euro to $1.24–1.35. If the dollar continues to depreciate, the possibilities for

Europeans to export goods to the United States will continue to deteriorate and the situation will rapidly become untenable.

It is evident that the country which issues the international reserve currency has at its disposal a formidable tool to finance its economy and service its public debt, to impose its financial conditions on the rest of the world, and to free itself from external constraint. What is the use of worrying about one's external deficits when it is possible to print dollars to pay one's suppliers? Being disconnected from gold, the dollar could be multiplied without an immediate automatic effect on its value or on inflation, which would permit Americans to have their growing commercial deficits financed indefinitely by the rest of the world, especially thanks to the issue of Treasury Bonds. In fact, the massive demand for dollars has permitted Americans to accumulate extravagant commercial and budget deficits without suffering any negative economic effects from the debts for a long time, which such imbalances should normally have provoked. The result is that the United States can live beyond its means thanks to foreign capital, and, for at least the last thirty years, the American economy has lived off the rest of the world. It fabricates a false growth, which provokes the regular increase of the stock indexes on the sole basis that money is accumulated in the investment portfolios, but which does not reflect any real economic development. The machine runs by generating debts that grow automatically.

In this system, where the fluctuation of the dollar immediately affects the whole of the international economy, the different countries of the world are constrained to buy the green bills issued by Washington to avoid any major imbalance, which allows the Americans to accumulate debts with total impunity, even while acquiring for themselves 80% of international savings. 'When it wishes to attract capital, as in the 1980s, [America] raises interest rates and causes its currency to climb; when it places its hopes on countries with low salaries, the low prices of their products largely compensates for the increasing prices of imported food products caused by currency differences. For America, it is a winning gamble. The deficits accumulate, but it is the emerging countries and Japan that pay.'[29]

But there is still a limit, and it has been reached today. The American public deficit is, in fact, henceforth out of control, with an explosion of expenses (up 41% in 2009 compared to 2008) and a collapse of fiscal revenues (down 28%). The federal deficit has reached almost 200 billion dollars for the month of March 2009 alone, or almost half of the total deficit recorded in 2008. Let us remember that the American budget deficit was still only 184 billion dollars in 1984. As for the public debt, it presently exceeds 14,000 billion dollars.

With all factors combined, the total debt of the United States now reaches 340% of its GDP, with private debt representing 170% of the GDP. If one relates this private American debt to America's effective production of primary and secondary goods, the Americans are indebted in the amount of approximately six years of industrial and agricultural production. The total debt is equivalent to twelve years of production. These are almost incredible figures which pose a clear problem to the other countries of the world, and primarily to China.

The total of Chinese reserves is today estimated at between 2,000 and 2,300 billion dollars, of which approximately 1,400 billion (roughly 70%) are held in American dollars (900 billion of Treasury Bonds, approximately 550 billion in other bonds, almost 200 billion in stocks, and 40 billion of short-term deposits), the remainder consisting mainly of stocks denominated in euros. Japan and other countries also possess important dollar reserves that they have accumulated as a result of penetrating the American market. With more than 550 billion dollars, the Eurozone comes in third — behind China and Japan, but before Russia and the Gulf states. Europe is thus among the biggest holders of reserves in dollars.

Until recently, a tacit agreement existed between Washington and Beijing. China continued to finance the American debt by re-injecting

---

29   Martine Bulard, 'Pékin, le dollar et le G20,' blog of *Le Monde diplomatique*, 31 March 2009.

its trade surpluses into the system by purchasing Treasury Bonds, while in return, the Americans opened their domestic market to Chinese products. China thus found itself in the situation of the rope that suspends the hanged man: in theory it held the American economy at its mercy, but if it made it collapse, it would at the same time hurt its own interests. And, if it decided to abruptly get rid of its dollars in preference for another currency judged to be more secure, a collapse of the dollar would ensue, rendering China's dollar assets worthless before they could be converted into other currencies. China would also run the risk of American retaliation, such as perhaps by the freezing of Chinese assets.

This tacit accord between China and the United States seems close to breaking. The message that Beijing conveyed to the directors of the G20 in 2009, on the eve of the London Summit, was clear. Through the governor of its central bank, Zhou Xiaochuan, China declared that 'the eruption of the crisis and its overflow throughout the world reflects the inherent vulnerabilities and the systemic risks of the international monetary system' of which the dollar is the pivot. The Chinese therefore explicitly demanded the replacement of the dollar as an international reserve currency with a 'supra-sovereign reserve currency', capable of 'remaining stable over the long term' and which would be 'dissociated from individual nations', clearly a currency based on a 'basket' of currencies including, apart from the dollar, the yuan, the euro, the rouble, and the riyal, something which the United States, of course, does not wish to hear mentioned.

With this declaration, which had the effect of a bombshell, China aimed first at preventing any challenge to its own currency, which is notoriously undervalued. It also intended to protect itself against a strong devaluation of the dollar, which would also devalue its enormous reserves, but above all to prepare for a total overhaul of the international financial system. More far-reaching than simply a new currency, it would entail a redistribution of the roles at the heart of the big organisations such as the International Monetary Fund (IMF) and the World Bank, where the Asians have never been able to obtain responsibilities proportionate to their economic power, nor to their demographic weight (China holds only 3.6% of the voting rights within the IMF, while the United States arrogates to itself 16.8%), as well as the transfer of the actual power of monetary creation currently held by the Federal Reserve to an international monetary fund.

The Chinese also evoke the possibility of resorting to the special drawing rights (SDRs), created in 1969, to attempt to limit the privileges of the dollar. The value of a SDR is determined on the basis of a 'basket' of currencies (the dollar, the pound, the yen, and the euro) in order to make of it a true reserve currency, a proposition that had been made by France already in 1964, but without any success. The utilisation of the SDR, which is today only a simple accounting unit for the operations of the IMF, has always been met with hostility by the Americans.

It also seems that China is now trying by all means to get rid of these 'toxic' assets that the American Treasury Bonds have become for them, by exchanging them for assets that they need on a long-term basis and which are today at historically low prices. Since the end of 2008, China has offloaded 50 to 100 billion of its dollar assets every month, totalling almost 600 billion dollars. China no longer buys more than a small amount of Treasury Bonds, and those generally being short-term bonds. It is estimated that, since the end of 2008, it has declined to buy between 500 to 1,000 billion dollars of Treasury Bonds, which the American administration sought to place on the international markets to finance its public deficits. With China no longer stepping up to meet the financing demands of the United States, the latter henceforth takes the risk of creating new money in order to avoid bankruptcy, entering in this way into the deadly spiral of inflation. On 18 March 2009 the Federal Reserve decided to purchase 300 billion dollars of Treasury Bonds. In the long run, this will inevitably lead to inflation.

Lately, there have been many signs that confirm the intentions of the Chinese. In the course of the last months, South Korea, Malaysia, Indonesia,

Belarus, Argentina, and Brazil have signed an exchange agreement with China, allowing their businesses to stop using the American dollar for their bilateral commercial exchanges. Moreover, China allows countries that are indebted to it to have their loans denominated in yuan instead of dollars. In April 2009, it became known that Chinese-American trade had decreased by 6.8% during the last year, while American investments in China fell by 19.4%. Some days later, the Chinese central bank announced that it had doubled its gold reserves.

Simultaneously, certain petroleum-producing countries envisage replacing their petro-dollars with petro-euros. Since 2007, the big Japanese oil refineries have begun to pay for Iranian crude petrol in yen. Around 65% of Iran's oil sales are now transacted in euros and the other 20% in yen. In April 2009, the Russian President, Dmitri Medvedev, also declared that he was for the creation of a new 'international and supra-national currency reserve', eventually to be placed under the aegis of the IMF. Some months earlier, in the beginning of February, the Russian finance minister, Alexei Kudrin, had already declared that 'the creation of an international monetary unit is a bold initiative that requires incomparable vision and courage ... In the short term, the international community, and in particular the IMF, would need to at least recognise the problem and deal with the risks resulting from the present system'. For their part, the central banks of South Korea, Taiwan, Russia, Syria, and Italy have announced plans to reduce their credit in dollars. In short, the policies of the American central bank are increasingly being contested. Yesterday, everybody wished to buy dollars — today, everybody wants to get rid of them.[30]

'The fate of the dollar is in the hands of Japan, China, and the Gulf states,' Jean-Pierre Chevènement[31] recently estimated. In fact, it is essentially in the hands of China. The Russians are less well-placed to contest the hegemony of the dollar, for their economy and their financial structures are

---

30 Cf. Cécile Prudhomme, 'L'hégémonie du dollar est attaqué de toutes parts', *Le Monde*, 7 June 2009.
31 'La voix de la France dans le monde', *Le Monde*, 22 October 2008.

not yet sufficiently solid. As for the euro, even though today it represents 26% of international monetary reserves, compared to 20% ten years ago, its position as an international currency has yet to be consolidated, to say the least. On the contrary, if China left the dollar system, the United States would immediately find itself in a state of bankruptcy.

On this question, one notes a deep division at the heart of the G20. The Americans and the British, followed by the Japanese, try to preserve the status quo with all their strength, while the Chinese, Russians, Indians, Brazilians, Argentineans, and South Africans openly campaigning for a far-reaching reform of the international financial system, while the Europeans, as usual, are incapable of breaking away.

For the moment, the United States is going to have to place between 1,700 and 1,900 billion dollars of Treasury Bonds a year on the financial markets. Who is going to buy them? Or, more precisely: what volume of Treasury Bonds will the Americans monetise by having the Federal Reserve purchase them, and what volume will the Chinese and the G20 countries agree to buy? We will soon know. On the other hand, it cannot be discounted that we may witness, more or less in the near future, the creation of new regional currencies by the non-Chinese holders of dollars. The multiplication of reserve currencies could give birth to new commercial regions. Another 'catastrophe scenario' would be the devaluing of the dollar far below a certain threshold, which would oblige all the central banks to stop supporting the American currency.[32]

George Soros said in January 2008, 'The world is rushing towards the end of the era of the dollar.' The problem is that it is only too evident that the United States will not renounce, of their own free will, the privileges of their currency. On the contrary, the Americans will do everything they can to continue to borrow from abroad, since their economy would otherwise collapse (let us not forget that they consume 800 billion dollars more each year than they produce). The real question is therefore whether the

---

32 Cf. Michel Aglietta and Laurent Berrebi, *Désordres dans le capitalisme mondial* (Paris: Odile Jacob, 2007).

Chinese will choose a path of confrontation with America. That is one of the big unknowns of the years to come.

Free Trade and Protectionism

When it was created in 1842, the very liberal Société d'économie politique[33] coined the slogan, 'Nobody is an economist if he is a protectionist.' That shows the extent to which, in liberal milieus, free trade was already at that time considered to be a factor contributing to 'progress.' Today, the situation is unchanged. Since the end of the Second World War, free trade has become the dominant economic doctrine. The creation of free trade zones such as the European Union, NAFTA (in North America), and the Mercosur (in South America) has been one of the consequences of the opening up of national economies. The World Trade Organization (WTO), which has been in operation from 1 January 1995, is also devoted to promoting free trade. In 1979, international sales of goods and services represented barely 12% of international GDP; today it represents almost 30%.

Free trade is based on the idea that rules and regulations should be the same everywhere, in order to arrive at 'pure and perfect' competition to the greatest possible extent, which permits the 'invisible hand' to exert its influence on every market. In the jargon of economists, its ideal is the 'level playing field' free from everything that might present an obstacle to the free play of the market: borders, controls, regulations, customs tariffs, and so on. From this perspective, the problem is not international trade,

---

[33] The Société d'économie politique is an economics society founded in Paris in 1842, based on the model of the Society of Political Economy in London. It advocates free trade and opposes protectionism. It still exists today.—Ed.

which is devoted to extending itself indefinitely, but the 'rigidity' of salaries and labour regulations, considered as curbing the competitiveness of developed countries. As for equal rules for everybody, the goal of free trade is ultimately the abolition of all rules, of everything that could impede the planetary expansion of the logic of credit and profit. Free trade is, in the final analysis, nothing but the absolute freedom of capital and its capacity to control the world, without submitting to any rules.

The general idea is that international trade represents the principal driving force of economic growth, and that we will therefore see more growth the more completely we suppress everything that might disturb trade. That is translated in reality into a general rush towards exports. The studies pertaining to the correlation between the degree of the opening up of economies and growth rates, however, do not confirm this idea. They show, on the contrary, that free trade does not necessarily result in an equalisation of prices across the board; but rather that if it benefits certain countries (generally the richest), it also seriously hurts others, for it induces deeply destructive distortions between countries endowed with different socio-productive systems, because adjustment of supply and demand does not happen at the same speed everywhere (the theorem of Mordecai Ezekiel).[34] Besides, it is inaccurate to depend only on the GDP (or gross national product [GNP]) to measure wealth, for these indices cannot, by definition, take into consideration goods and services traded off-exchange. 'The *commodification* of an economy which initially possesses a non-mercantile sector,' recalls Jacques Sapir, 'is always translated into a rise of the GDP, even when the real wealth of the country diminishes.'[35]

The economists, blinded by their adherence to the dogmas of economic liberalism, are in fact incapable of thinking of the collective dimension,

---

34 Mordecai Ezekiel (1899–1974) was an American economist who worked on agricultural policy during the Franklin Roosevelt administration, and later for the United Nations. Ezekiel observed the fluctuations between supply and prices in the American pork market, and his explanatory model came to be known as the 'pork cycle.'—Ed.

35 'Le protectionnisme aujourd'hui', paper read at the Conference on the Crisis of International Free Trade organised on 27 April 2009 in Paris by the Fondation Res Publica.

the national or continental entities, or the phenomena of influence and power that always get in the way of 'pure and perfect' competition. They also refuse to admit that it is not consumption (demand) which is the goal of economic growth (supply), but economic growth which is the fruit of consumption. Moreover, they do not see that the system of supply and demand, which is supposed to adjust itself spontaneously, can at best satisfy only the *solvent* demand, which is rapidly diminishing. They imagine that the liberalisation or total deregulation of trade will allow all participants to benefit equally from their commercial relations, when, in fact, inequalities grow steadily worse, both between and within countries. The principle of 'free and undistorted' competition is a contradiction in terms: every 'free' competition is necessarily distorted, and every undistorted competition is no longer 'free'.

The Nobel Prize-winner Maurice Allais[36] recalled this a long time ago, stating in 1988: 'A liberalisation of all exchanges and movements of capitals is possible and desirable only within the scope of regional groups uniting countries which are economically and politically related, and with comparable economic and social development.'[37] In other words, free trade is only possible between socio-productive systems endowed with similar structures. That is why 'total liberalisation of trade on the international level, the stated objective of the World Trade Organization, must be considered at once unrealisable, harmful, and undesirable.'[38]

As regards international trade, free-tradeism is also based on the theory of 'comparative advantage' enunciated by David Ricardo.[39] This theory, according to which every country has an interest in specialising in the production of those goods in which it is most competitive, is based on the im-

---

36 Maurice Allais (1911–2010) was a French economist who won the Nobel Memorial Prize in Economics in 1988. He was critical of the euro and believed that many nations were guilty of creating money out of nothing.—Ed.

37 Maurice Allais, *La mondialisation: la destruction des emplois et de la croissance* (Paris: Clément Juglar, 1999).

38 Cf. Maurice Allais, 'L'éclatante faillite du nouveau credo', *Le Figaro*, 27 December 2009.

39 David Ricardo (1772–1823) was a British political economist. He outlined his theory of comparative advantage in his 1817 book, *On the Principles of Political Economy and Taxation*.—Ed.

plicit idea that economies are defined by constant returns on scale, which does not correspond to reality. A country that is extremely specialised and focuses heavily on exports will, in reality, soon find itself in a position where it is unable to satisfy its domestic demand, and becomes dependent on fluctuating exchange rates that it does not master. By abandoning the productive sectors in which it is considered to be less competitive, it also abandons an expertise, an 'intangible resource', which will impede the future development of its entire economy.

Of course, this anti-protectionist dogma is also very hypocritical. The United States, the big promoter of free trade, has never hesitated, as everyone knows, to take recourse (by devaluation, direct or indirect subsidies, customs duties, etc.) to protectionism every time they consider it to be in their interest to do so. The Americans, in particular, finance their military-industrial complex through public purchasing. And the Chinese massively subsidise their exports when they manipulate their currency in order to inundate the Western markets with cheap products, and so on.

Globalisation, which has sparked the spectacular economic take-off of emerging countries (China, India, Brazil, etc.) we have seen since 2000, has combined three factors: the progressive lowering of customs barriers, the deregulation of financial markets, and technological advances in communication and transport. The extension of free trade has gone hand in hand with globalisation, favouring the free circulation of labour, goods, and capital. This has facilitated the outsourcing of industry to emerging countries with little technological competence but extremely low wages, as well as massive exports of cheap goods originating in countries which, like China, essentially base their growth on external demand, and support their exports by keeping their currencies undervalued. Such countries have virtually unlimited reservoirs of manpower at their disposal, at salaries 30 to 80 times lower than those of Western countries. These extremely low salaries are, of course, a 'comparative advantage' for developing countries, but constitute unfair competition for those who suffer as a result of them.

Globalisation has allowed the bourgeoisie and the local ruling strata to deterritorialise production in the hope of freeing themselves from the constricting frameworks of nations and states, by transplanting a growing part of this production to regions of the planet that are the least conscientious in such matters as salaries, taxation, social security, and environmental protection. This development results in growing social costs. Free trade, in fact, breaks the equilibrium between production and consumption. By placing countries at completely different economic levels and with different social structures in competition on an equal footing, it creates dumping conditions and unbearable social distortions. It leads businesses to consider their wage-earners as nothing but a cost and, in reducing their salaries, pushes them into brutal, inhumane competition.

The globalisation and deregulation processes initiated in the 1980s, which reached its height in the middle of the 1990s, has not only dug an ever deeper ditch between the financial system and the real economy. It has caused the surplus value of production to be increasingly allocated to shareholders and holders of capital while wage-earners receive less.[40] By exposing the workforces of developed countries to competition from the underpaid labourers of emerging economies, capital owners have managed to depress salaries, forgetting that workers are also consumers.

In this sense, globalisation has indeed marked the end of the Fordist system in which it was in the interest of capital to regularly increase the remuneration of wage-earners in order to maximise their capacity for consumption. The increase of production and consumption thus went hand-in-hand. This 'virtuous circle' was broken the moment that, in order to satisfy the demands of free trade, it was necessary to reduce salaries with the sole aim of remaining 'competitive' in relation to countries where similar goods can be produced, but at much lower wages. Increasingly subject to

---

40 In the United States, the share of work compensation in the national revenue fell by 51.6% in 2006, its lowest point historically since 1929, whereas, from 2000 to 2007, the proportion of inhabitants deprived of all social security climbed to 15.6%. In Mexico, the average salary per household has stagnated since the creation of NAFTA. It has remained the same for the last fifteen years in the majority of developed countries.

shareholder pressure — shareholders demanding maximum returns on investments, which implies redundancies, reduction of salaries, outsourcing, and so on — wage-earners have had to accept increasingly worse working conditions in order to keep their jobs. (In many countries having social structures similar to those of France, the total cost of illness due to work-related stress already represents close to 3% of the GDP.) Their standard of living began to decrease, while unemployment increased. The gap between the average income and the median income grew wider. The deflation of salaries has led to a relative impoverishment of the working and middle classes, and thus to a relative weakening of domestic demand. While most governments undertook 'reforms', the concerned parties were well aware that those reforms consisted essentially in making them work more while earning less.[41]

Under these conditions, the political and sociological capacity to increase the demand for goods and services has not stopped falling, even though the technological and economic capacity to offer goods and services has continued to grow. This is thanks in particular to productivity gains, of which one of the consequences is to increase unemployment, these gains allowing the production of increasingly more goods with increasingly fewer men, and making work at the same time a rare commodity. (Since 2005, the International Labour Office remarked that there was increasingly less correlation between economic growth and the creation of jobs.)

The principal result of the expansion of free trade, beyond the immediate marginal benefits that might have resulted from it (economies of scale, more efficient allocation of certain factors of production, etc.), has thus been decreasing growth rates coupled with a very strong rise of economic

---

41 Jacques Sapir, for his part, points out that 'the combination of free trade and the monetary rigidity of the euro makes illegal immigration necessary, from the point of view of businesses. The illegal immigrant is not covered by existing labour laws. Immigration then becomes the equivalent of a *de facto* devaluation and a dismantlement of labour laws under the pressure of imported competition' ('Le retour du protectionnisme et la fureur de ses ennemis,' *Le monde diplomatique*, March 2009, p. 19).

inequality in all countries.[42] The only way to compensate for the decreasing growth resulting from the deflation of salaries, lack of social security, and the consequent decrease in internal demand has been through borrowing. When salaries stagnate and workers are underpaid, demand can only arise from borrowing and credit. Threatened with impoverishment, wage-earners go into ever greater debt to try to maintain their standard of living, even though their real incomes diminish. When they have reached a certain threshold, they become unable to repay their debts, and the entire system runs the risk of collapse. This is what happened in the fall of 2008 when the American 'subprime' crisis initiated the present international crisis. The boom in credit mechanisms resulting from the attempt to artificially maintain the consumption capacity of households through credit, even while their real incomes stagnated or diminished, finally culminated in a widespread crisis in the private sector (encompassing households as well as businesses).

This crisis has broken out in the United States because it is a country where one consumes more than one produces, and savings there are nonexistent. Their incomes diminishing, the Americans were destined to become indebted, and this indebtedness has reached heights never seen before. From 2007, the debt of American households represented 100% of the GDP![43] After the United States, the countries most affected have been those with the highest debts, and those inspired by the Anglo-Saxon model of a very open and financialised economy: England and Spain first of all, but also the Netherlands, Ireland, Hungary, and South Korea. Several other countries today are practically bankrupt: Ireland, Greece, Iceland, Ukraine, and Romania.

Emmanuel Todd very correctly observes that the negative effects of free trade are rising from the bottom to the top of society. In the 1980s, it was

---

42 'The fundamental mechanism of free trade,' declares Emmanuel Todd, 'is the introduction into every country of the inequalities that exist at the international level, and thus the squeezing of salaries' (interview with Karim Emile Bitar, *L'Ena hors les murs*, April 2009).

43 In France, at the same time, the debt of households equalled 47.6% of the GDP.

the workers who were most affected by the increasing inequalities. Then, in the 1990s, the decline hit the middle classes, who began suffering the effects of impoverishment and the consequent loss of social position. Today, the profits of free trade benefit only the top 1% of society, who become ever richer, while the gaps in salaries widen and the mass of wage-earners become increasingly poorer. 'The adherence of the elites to free trade,' says Emmanuel Todd, 'henceforth causes society as a whole to suffer.'[44]

The most threatened groups are no longer the least qualified, as in the past, but those whose jobs are easiest to outsource to other countries. The champions of free trade could not care less about that, outsourcing being justified in their eyes solely because it increases competitiveness, and thus allows capital owners to acquire a still larger share of the wealth produced. (It is the same argument which was used to justify child labour in the nineteenth century.) 'I am proud of being a boss who outsources,' Guillaume Sarkozy, President of the Union des industries textiles (UIT) and the brother of we-know-who, recently declared.[45]

Whether directly or indirectly, already realised or used as a threat to blame labour agreements and social regulations acquired through struggle in the past, the outsourcing of businesses first affected the low-end products of mass consumption. Then, from the late 1980s, consumer electronics, electrical household appliances and cars, and finally, since the middle of the 1990s, also the most sophisticated products as well as 'intangible' services (information processing, interpretation of radiological examinations, etc.) were hit. The distance between the places of production and consumption has thus become increasingly greater.

Contrary to the generally held view, the predatory policies of emerging countries have not only had a devastating effect on the economies of developed countries, but have also destabilised the countries of the Third World. Developing countries have in fact gained little from the rules of

---

44 Emmanuel Todd, 'Vive le protectionnisme!', *Le Nouvel Observateur*, 30 October 2008, p. 112.
45 *L'Expansion*, 28 November 2002.

the World Trade Organization. 'Contrary to what is often claimed', writes Jacques Sapir, 'free trade has not been a positive factor in the development of the poorest countries, and its effect on the reduction of poverty has been greatly overestimated, when it has not been the product of errors of calculation.'[46] The argument according to which the imbalances that one notes today profit, more or less, the populations of less developed nations is thus contestable, since the inequalities between countries continue to increase. In fact, the gains realised in the emerging countries serve above all to enrich a small ruling segment of society whose fortunes have literally exploded in the course of the last ten years.

The risk today is of a deflationary spiral arising from a dramatic increase in unemployment and a general lowering of incomes, but also from a strong decline in industrial production in the developed countries. Already in 1999, Maurice Allais, in his book *La crise mondiale d'aujourd'hui*, predicted the 'general collapse' of an 'international economy based entirely on a pyramid of debts'. We are approaching that point.

***

Since the present international economic crisis broke out, all the leaders of the planet declare that they are ready to take 'drastic' measures to deal with the 'urgency' and the gravity of the situation. But at the same time they vie with one another in declaring — one saw it in April 2009 during the G20 meeting in London, and at the more recent Italian summit — that the principle of globalisation should not be questioned, and that it is necessary to fight against all forms of protectionism. The main reason for this attitude is that they think the crisis comes down to financial deregulation, and that it would be sufficient to purge to guarantee a return to normalcy. In actuality, however, it is also a consequence of the real economy and derives from the very nature itself of the dominant economic system.

---

46 Jacques Sapir, 'De l'avenir du protectionnisme: Les leçons des années 1930 pour comprendre la crise actuelle', *Les Cahiers de l'indépendance*, January 2009, p. 159.

Denounced by the leaders of states and governments, protectionism is also rejected on the Right (and on the extreme Right) by liberals who are loyal to the free-trade dogma, but also by a large part of the Left and the extreme Left, Trotskyists in particular, for whom the problem of protectionism clashes strongly with their internationalist convictions. (In the last European elections, as Jacques Sapir has remarked, the party of Olivier Besancenot[47] was the only one to refuse to address this problem in any way whatsoever. As for the Socialist Party, which thinks it can resolve the problems by limiting itself to fighting for a more 'social' Europe, it considers protectionism a taboo subject.)[48] In a more general way, it is the entire New Class,[49] of the Right and the Left, which never tires of thundering against the 'protectionist menace,' the very words 'barriers', 'protection', 'regulation', and so on becoming for them synonymous with isolationism, nationalism, and even xenophobia.[50] Obviously, for the free-trade ideology, protectionism is the devil. And that goes even beyond simple economics. From a symbolic point of view, in fact, protectionism is a barrier against unlimited change, a measure against immoderation, the 'earthly' element as opposed to the 'liquid' element.

'The refusal to identify free trade as a cause of the present distress,' writes Jacques Sapir, 'shows that its champions have abandoned the universe of reflection to enter into that of magical thought.'[51]

In France, Jacques Sapir is probably the one who argues most vigorously for a return to protectionism. He is not the only one. Emmanuel

---

47 The Nouveau parti anticapitaliste (New Anticapitalist Party).—Ed.

48 In a text dated 18 May 2009 which was circulated on the Internet under the title 'Vous avez la parole ... mais à condition de dire ce que nous avons envie d'entendre' [You may speak ... but on condition that you say what we want to hear], Jacques Sapir has related how, at the end of an interview that he had given to the internal bulletin of the PS [Socialist Party], he was told that his own doubts about a 'socialist Europe' could not be published. His response was to cancel the publication. Sapir speaks of it as an 'example of liberal Stalinism'. Cf. also François Denord and Antoine Schwartz, *L'Europe sociale n'aura pas lieu* (Paris: Raisons d'agir, 2009).

49 The idea of the New Class was coined in the 1970s to describe new political classes which were arising that were driven to effect political and social change for reasons other than those based on economic necessity.—Ed.

50 Cf. François Ruffin, 'On ne peut pas desserrer l'étau, ou on ne veut pas?', *Le Monde diplomatique*, March 2009, pp. 20–21.

51 'Le retour du protectionnisme et la fureur de ses ennemis', *Le Monde diplomatique*, p. 18.

Todd, who had already denounced free-tradeism in *L'illusion économique* (The Economic Illusion),[52] develops anew the same arguments in his latest work, *Après la démocratie* (After Democracy).[53] He is joined in the defence of protectionism by Hakim El Karoui and Jean-Luc Gréau.[54] El Karoui, Sapir, and Gréau were, besides, all present at the conference on the crisis of international free trade organised by the Fondation Res Publica on 27 April 2009 in Paris under the presidency of Jean-Pierre Chevènement. Some economists of international renown are also beginning to rally to the idea of protectionism, such as the strongly neoclassical Paul Samuelson, who recently observed that the Chinese case made Ricardo's old theory of comparative advantage untenable. As for public opinion, all studies published in recent years show that protectionism is supported by the majority of Europeans, especially in France, where 73% of the people think that globalisation represents a threat to employment.[55] 'The mood is rather for protectionism', noted the newspaper *Les Echos* twelve years ago.[56]

'Contrary to all liberal thought', observes Laurent Cohen-Tanugi, 'globalisation cannot today be separated from the return of geopolitics with a vengeance, or from power strategies, nationalisms, even historic empires ... This return is heavy with consequences, primarily of an ideological nature: the depoliticisation of economic movements, a dogma of liberal globalisation since the 1980s, is going to come up increasingly against the geopoliticisation of the international economic space resulting from the economic take-off of continent-sized nations legitimately animated by strategic ambition.'[57]

---

52 Emmanuel Todd, *L'illusion économique: Essai sur la stagnation des sociétés développées* (Paris: Gallimard, 1998).

53 Emmanuel Todd, *Après la démocratie* (Paris: Gallimard, 2008).

54 Cf. Hakim El Karoui, *L'avenir d'une exception* (Paris: Flammarion, 2006); and Jean-Luc Gréau, *La trahison des économistes* (Paris: Gallimard, 2008).

55 Sofres survey, February 2005.

56 *Les Echos*, 8 January 1997.

57 'La mondialisation n'est plus ce qu'elle était,' *Les Echos*, 13 March 2007.

The anti-protectionist arguments themselves are not new. Protectionism is still accused of encouraging 'isolationism', of causing a contraction of international trade, of creating unfair privileges by instituting systems of production artificially protected from the positive effects of competition, of weakening the purchasing power of the poorest through higher prices of protected products, and so on. But the big argument is historical: it consists in a biased evocation of the protectionism instituted in the 1930s, which is claimed to have aggravated the effects of the depression of 1929, and, in the end, to have led to war. As the present crisis is everywhere being compared to 1929, the conclusion would seem to follow automatically.

In the United States, the adoption of the famous Smoot-Hawley Tariff Act, which was signed into law by President Herbert Hoover on 17 June 1930, resulted in the establishment of customs tariffs of up to 52% on more than 20,000 products. Three years later, the total production of the country had fallen by 27%, while the imports had decreased by 34% and the exports by 46%. More than 60 countries had then raised their customs tariffs or set up quotas. The global volume of international trade fell by 40% between 1929 and 1932. Liberal economists conclude from this that these measures only aggravated the crisis: the closing of the borders is said to have provoked the implosion of international trade before leading to war. That is why protectionism was so strongly stigmatised during the Bretton Woods conference in July 1944, which laid the foundations for post-war free-tradeism.

As we have said, this argument is biased. That has already been shown by Paul Bairoch who, in *Mythes et paradoxes de l'histoire économique* (Myths and Paradoxes of Economic History),[58] indicated that international trade did not decline at the same pace as the production of the countries concerned, and that the decline in international trade could therefore not have caused the Depression. The same demonstration has been made more recently by Jacques Sapir in a text dated 8 January 2009 entitled, 'Will the

---

58   Paul Bairoch, *Mythes et paradoxes de l'histoire économique* (Paris: La Découverte, 2005).

Present Crisis Lead to War? False and True Lessons from the 1930s'. In it Sapir recalls that 'the essential part of the contraction of trade took place between January 1930 and July 1932, that is, before the institution of protectionist, or autarchic, measures in certain countries'.[59] Besides, if the share of exports of goods in the GDP of the big, industrialised countries indeed moved from 9.8% to 6.2% between 1929 and 1938, we must remember that it was only 12.9% in 1913. The champions of free trade also forget that, in the 1930s, international trade consisted essentially of raw materials, which then represented two-thirds of such trade, whereas today two-thirds of international trade consists of manufactured goods. In fact, the real cause of the collapse of international trade in the 1930s was not protectionism, but the sharp rise in the costs of transport and delivery, the widespread disorganisation of the financial system which followed the accumulation of 'competitive' devaluations decided on after the mistake of the London Economic Conference[60] in 1933, and the contraction of international liquidity (which fell by 35.7% in 1930 and 26.7% in 1931), which resulted in a crisis of demand ending in what John Maynard Keynes[61] called 'the balance of underemployment'.[62] As for the Smoot-Hawley Tariff Act, it only made the level of protectionism in the world rise marginally.

It was his consideration of this crisis of the 1930s which made Keynes realise the importance of feeding the international system with liquidity, and led him, who had until then been rather favourable to free trade, to consider that free trade had no more benefits to offer, and to declare himself increasingly in favour of protectionism, notably in his famous article of

---

59 In another version of the same text, Sapir emphasises in the passage that 'Nazism is not a radicalisation of German nationalism of the period of Wilhelm II, but its negation' ('De l'avenir du protectionisme', p. 161).

60 The London Economic Conference was held in June and July 1933, in part in the hope that the United States would lead the recovery effort by enacting currency stabilisation and fixing the dollar at a high value, which would improve the prospects for trade from the European powers into the US, although this was opposed by most Americans, who wanted a devaluation of the dollar to improve America's own advantage in trade. President Roosevelt ultimately rejected the European proposal.—Ed.

61 John Maynard Keynes (1883–1946) was a British economist whose ideas regarding the the possibilities of the free market and business cycles have been extraordinarily influential.—Ed.

62 Cf. also Jean-Marc Vittori, 'Les fausses leçons de la crise de 1929', *Les Echos*, 26 February 2009.

1933, 'National Self-Sufficiency'.[63] Keynes writes there, 'The decadent international but individualistic capitalism, in the hands of which we found ourselves after the [Great] War, is not a success. It is not intelligent, it is not beautiful, it is not just, it is not virtuous — and it doesn't deliver the goods.'

American production in 1938 was still inferior to that of 1929. It is, we know, the war effort that would make the relaunching of the machine possible, at the cost of an explosion of public debt, which would not stop increasing. One may ask oneself if it is not actually the obstinate refusal of the capitalist system to be limited that even today risks leading to war (with Iran, for example). There comes a moment when capital, confronted with the tendential lowering of its profit rates and the impossibility of finding new outlets, can only bank on war to find a new stimulus, first in the form of armaments production, and then in the reconstruction following the massive devastation caused by the conflict.

Another tactic of free-tradeists consists in denouncing protectionism at the national level. Then they do not have any difficulty in showing that protectionism would today be both impossible to establish and inefficient. The nation-states, in terms of financial fluxes and exchange of goods, are no longer equal to the international economy. It was not always so. In the past, protectionism was incontestably a necessity for emerging countries wishing to build, free from competition that they were not yet in a position to face, industries destined to confront international competition at a later stage. Friedrich List (1789–1846)[64] was one of the first theoreticians of such protectionism.[65] For List, who was not anti-liberal — his positions are clearly distinct from those adopted before him by Fichte[66] in *The Closed*

---

[63] *The Yale Review*, vol. 22, no. 4 (June 1933), pp. 755–769. Cf. also H. E. Daly, 'The Perils of Free Trade', *Scientific American*, November 1933.

[64] Friedrich List was a German philosopher and economist, and the author of *International System of Political Economy*. He has never been translated into English.—Ed.

[65] Cf. his *The National System of Political Economy*, trans. Sampson S. Lloyd (New York: Augustus M. Kelley, 1966), originally published in 1841.

[66] Johann Gottlieb Fichte (1762–1814) was one of the principal philosophers of German Idealism, which grew out of Immanuel Kant's ideas. Some have claimed that the type of state Fichte advocated in this book resembles modern-day dictatorships.—Ed.

Commercial State[67] — protectionism represented an arsenal of transitory measures allowing the attainment of the threshold from which competition between countries could be exercised on an undistorted basis. He was not wrong: the economic rise of all the big industrial countries, beginning with the United States and Japan, began within the framework of protected markets from which investment strategies could be developed.[68]

But that does not mean that protectionism is only of temporary use, and that it should be reserved for countries that cannot yet pay for the luxury of free trade (it is always indispensable to protect strategically important industries, for example). Today, the question is whether to establish protectionism at the European continental level. This furnishes a response to the argument that protectionism would henceforth be 'impossible' because there are practically no longer any strictly national products, by virtue of the international fragmentation of the processes of production and the geographic dispersal of subcontracting, which results in one part of a car or a plane being manufactured in one country, another part in another country, and so on.

A canal lock is not a dam: it does not prevent the water from flowing, but allows its level to be regulated. Similarly, protectionism is not autarky. It is not the institution of insurmountable walls transforming states into so many impenetrable fortresses. In a Europe that is primarily threatened by wage deflation and outsourcing, the first objective of protectionism would be to allow internal demand to recover. Only a protected Europe can revive demand through salaries. As Jacques Sapir writes, 'to increase salaries without touching free trade is either hypocrisy or stupidity'.[69] For Europe, it is a question of becoming a space of economic regulation protecting itself

---

67 See Johann G.ottlieb Fichte, *The Closed Commercial State*, trans. Anthony Curtis Adler (Albany: State University of New York Press, 2012), originally published in 1800.—Ed.

68 Cf. especially Ha-Joon Chang, *Kicking Away the Ladder* (London: Anthem Press, 2002); Ha-Joon Chang, 'Du protectionnisme au libre-échangisme, une conversion opportuniste', *Le monde diplomatique* (June 2003); and Erik S. Reinert, *How Rich Countries Got Rich and Why Poor Countries Stay Poor* (London: Constable, 2007).

69 'Le retour du protectionisme et la fureur de ses ennemis', *Le Monde diplomatique*, p. 19.

from the most harmful effects of economic and financial globalisation in the form of price dumping and outsourcing to low-income countries, and of imposing a rule of reciprocity in international trade.

Only a system of commercial protection and of 'compensatory duties' can put an end to the devaluation and underpayment of work and cause internal demand to rise again, by controlling the exchanges of goods and services in such a way that European economies are no longer penalised by the *de facto* opportunities offered to countries whose social and environmental conditions of production differ radically from ours. The raising of salaries and the revival of demand through consumption can only be accomplished by adopting measures of customs protection, at the same time compensating for the losses that could eventually result from the closure of certain foreign markets.

Regarding commercial matters, one can certainly imagine a new common customs tariff, but this system risks running into the difficulty of fixing the exact level of compensatory tariffs in the present system of fluctuating exchange rates. The exchange rates between the dollar, the euro, and the yen vary constantly, and a customs duty on imported products could therefore rapidly be rendered ineffective. That is why the best system remains the one recommended by Maurice Allais, which is based on import quotas, which could possibly be auctioned out. From the moment that, for example, Chinese textile manufacturers exceed their quota of imports, they would have to pay a certain sum of money to the European Union, or move production facilities to Europe in order to create jobs there. Another solution could be to set up an anti-dumping tax, as already exists for certain products (for example, on bicycles imported from China).

But protectionist measures need not be reduced to customs tariffs and import quotas. They can also include laws limiting the investments of foreign enterprises, subsidies to producers or buyers, devaluations, social or fiscal measures, the establishment of technological and sanitary standards, safeguard clauses, and so forth. To remedy the heterogeneity of national economies in Europe, Jacques Sapir also advocates a return to the compensatory monetary sums adopted in the 1960s, which would allow the creation of a fund in which social and ecological needs would converge at the heart of the European Union.

Finally, protectionism must go beyond purely negative measures. To begin with, it could help stop the outsourcing of production, since having markets closer by will lower the costs and the environmental risks that outsourcing causes at the planetary level (for example, almost all gherkins consumed in France are today produced in India; Chinese strawberries are much cheaper than the strawberries from Périgord, but 20 times more petroleum is used for their transportation!) which may also allow for better quality control of products. It could also lead to the establishment of a veritable European sovereignty in industrial matters, thanks to a reinforcement of cooperation between big industrial actors, which could agree on common strategies in matters of production and the conquest of foreign markets. Protectionism, in a word, is the adoption of a preference for the European Community in all fields.

The objective being to generalise the principle of *self-centred* economies and to 'regulate commercial exchanges by imagining large geographic zones of sufficiently important size to avoid the creation of vested interests — the risk of protectionism — while making of it a means of organising the world',[70] there is evidently a strong congruence between a protectionism organised at the continental level and the movement towards a multipolar world, where the different poles would also play a regulatory role in relation to the globalisation in process. Protectionism, in this sense, is not only an economic weapon, but also a political weapon which permits the imposition of borders on a sphere of influence or on a cultural and civilisational bloc. As Raphaël Wintrebert has written, '"Commercial politics" is,

---

70   Hakim El Karoui, 'Les avantages d'un protectionnisme européen', delivered at the Conference on the Crisis of International Free Trade, Fondation Res Publica, Paris, 27 April 2009.

above all, politics and thus cannot be reduced to technical issues reserved for experts.'[71]

The adoption of these measures hardly poses any particular technical problem. But it comes up against the total lack of will on the part of European leaders. The most determined champions of free trade are found in the European Commission, at the heart of multinational corporations, the World Bank, and the IMF. Apart from its Common Agricultural Policy, Europe is today the 'free trade continent in a protectionist world'.[72] This free-tradeist orientation has dominated from the beginning, since the Treaty of Rome of 1957 already foresaw the 'progressive elimination of restrictions of international trade'. The Treaty of Amsterdam of 1997 even went so far as to abrogate the only article (44[2]) of the Treaty of Rome referring to 'natural preference'. Today, the 'Community preference' is considered to contradict the clauses of the European treaties as well as the commitments made to the World Trade Organization. This is why Europe, in recent years, has been the best pupil of the free-tradeism advocated by the WTO: at the heart of the European Union, the total of customs duties represents no more than 2% of the total value of trade (which, to cite but one example, has led to a trade deficit in relation to China of more than 80%). The official doctrine of the European Union is to accept the disappearance of a certain number of labour-intensive industries to concentrate instead on industries with high added value, but which employ few people. Under these conditions, the jobs created in the innovative sectors clearly cannot compensate for the jobs lost in the sectors which are abandoned. That is why the European Union has never been able to distinguish clearly between market and non-market activities, or to determine if it should or should not protect itself against competition that proves to be destructive

---

71 Raphaël Wintrebert, *Libre-échange, protectionnisme: comment sortir d'un faux dilemma?* (Paris: Fondation pour l'innovation publique, 2007), p. 3.

72 Guillaume Bachelay, 'Protectionnisme, ouvrons le débat!', *Marianne*, 27 February 2009.

for its member states. It is not surprising, then, that its industry steadily declines and that its middle classes sink into poverty.

Emmanuel Todd does not hesitate to say that the future will be either protectionism or chaos — or protectionism following chaos. For his part, Jean-Luc Gréau considers that 'The return of a new protectionism is inevitable.'[73] As for Jacques Sapir, he writes, 'In view of the crisis which is developing today, the combination of protectionism and a return to control systems on capitals, such as would stabilise the convertibility of currencies on the basis of commercial transactions of goods and services alone appears to be the basis for any solution, as was the case after the crisis of the 1930s. But, as in 1944, such a position can only run into the opposition of the United States... The defence of economic sovereignty is not compatible with the objectives of American policy... There can therefore be no reform and no way out of the crisis except on the basis of a confrontation with American policy.'[74]

The unanimous minds of the New Class will nevertheless continue to rage against the protectionist devil, regularly described as the 'worst of solutions' (Jean-Marie Colombani) and the 'deadly poison of the economy' (Claude Imbert). Observing this unanimity, Emmanuel Todd finds it easy to show that the true obstacle to protectionism lies in an ideological state of mind that can be described as libertarian-liberal: narcissism, individualism, obsession with money, and blatant contempt for the people. 'For me,' he declares, 'ultra-individualism is not a primordial adherence to the market economy, to the rejection of all customs barriers; it is an adherence to the idea of the individual as absolute monarch, to the idea that it is forbidden to forbid,[75] to that phenomenon of narcissisation of behaviours analysed

---

73 *Libération*, 9 July 2007.
74 'De l'avenir du protectionnisme', p. 165.
75 'It is forbidden to forbid' was one of the slogans of the protesters during the May 1968 unrest in France.—Ed.

by [Christopher] Lasch,[76] something extremely massive and diffuse at the same time ... The big heavy negative factor is this atomisation, this narcissisation of behaviours, this very heavy bias against collective action.'[77] But this individualism is, in fact, an individuo-universalism, and universalism is also consonant with free trade to the extent that it is classified under the idea of 'a world without borders', where nations will inevitably be 'superseded'. Todd also notes that, 'On the international level, universalism and anti-racism are directly related to the domination of free trade. The idea of opening up, of overcoming all differences, leads to that.'[78]

Protectionist legislation is certainly only a corrective to, and a version of, the market economy, not an alternative to the market economy. It does not fundamentally challenge all the prerogatives of capital, or the power relations in business. Protectionism is for this reason a reformism. In the present conditions, one is led to it by a concern to avoid the worst.

---

76 This is a reference to historian and moral philosopher Lasch's bestselling book, *The Culture of Narcissism: American Life in an Age of Diminishing Expectations* (New York: Norton, 1979), in which he analysed the roots and causes of the extreme forms of individualism in America.—Ed.

77 Interview with Karim Emile Bitar.

78 *Ibid.*

Death on Credit[79]

Ezra Pound writes in Canto XLV of his famous *Cantos*:

> With usura hath no man a house of good stone
>
> each block cut smooth and well fitting
>
> that delight might cover their face,
>
> with usura
>
> hath no man a painted paradise on his church wall
>
> ...
>
> with usura, sin against nature,
>
> is thy bread ever more of stale rags
>
> is thy bread dry as paper,
>
> with no mountain wheat, no strong flour
>
> with usura the line grows thick
>
> with usura is no clear demarcation
>
> and no man can find site for his dwelling
>
> Stone cutter is kept from his stone
>
> weaver is kept from his loom
>
> ...
>
> Corpses are set to banquet
>
> at behest of usura.[80]

---

[79] *Death on Credit* is the title of a novel by Louis-Ferdinand Céline, entitled *Death on the Installment Plan* in its English translation. The novel is about a doctor who treats the poor in spite of the fact that he is rarely paid for his work.—Ed.

[80] Ezra Pound, *New Selected Poems and Translations* (New York: New Directions, 2010), pp. 184–185.—Ed.

The excesses of lending at interest were condemned in Rome, as is testified to by Cato.[81] He considered that since those who steal sacred objects deserve double punishment, usurers deserve quadruple. Aristotle, in his condemnation of chrematistics,[82] is even more radical: 'There are two sorts of wealth-getting', he writes, 'as I have said; one is a part of household management, the other is retail trade: the former necessary and honourable, while that which consists in exchange is justly censured; for it is unnatural, and a mode by which men gain from one another. The most hated sort, and with the greatest reason, is usury, which makes a gain out of money itself, and not from the natural object of it. For money was intended to be used in exchange, but not to increase at interest. And this term interest, which means the birth of money from money, is applied to the breeding of money because the offspring resembles the parent. This is why of all modes of getting wealth this is the most unnatural' (*The Politics*).[83]

The word 'interest' designates revenue from money (*foenus* or *usura* in Latin, *tókos* in Greek). It relates to the way in which money 'has children'. From the High Middle Ages, the Church repeated in its turn the distinction that Roman law had made regarding the loan of chattels: there are things that are consumed through use and things that are not consumed, of which the latter are called *commodatum*. Demanding payment for the use of the latter is contrary to the common good, for money is not a good which is consumed. Lending at interest was condemned by the Council of Nicaea[84] on the basis of scripture — even though the Bible does not explicitly condemn it! In the twelfth century, the Church repeated in its turn the Aristotelian condemnation of chrematistics. Thomas Aquinas also condemned lending at interest, with some small reservations, on the principle

---

81 Cato the Elder (234–149 BCE) was a conservative Roman statesman. As Praetor of Rome he was a harsh opponent of usury, and usurers themselves were banished during his reign.—Ed.

82 The study of wealth, in terms of money.—Ed

83 Aristotle, *The Politics*, Book I, in *The Politics, and Constitution of Athens*, p. 25.—Ed.

84 The First Council of Nicea was a conference of bishops convened by Constantin I in 325 with the intention of creating a unified Christian doctrine for the first time.—Ed.

that 'time belongs only to God'. Islam, still more severe, does not even make a distinction between usury and interest.

The practice of lending at interest, however, gradually developed hand-in-hand with the rise of the bourgeois class and the expansion of mercantile values, which it made its instrument of power. From the fifteenth century, banks, commercial companies, and then the manufacturers, could grant loans through a special dispensation from the king. An essential turning point corresponded to the appearance of Protestantism, and more precisely of Calvinism. Jean Calvin was the first theologian to accept the practice of lending at interest, which then expanded by means of the banking networks. With the French Revolution, lending at interest became entirely free, while new banks appeared in large numbers, endowed with considerable funds which were coming particularly from speculation on national goods.[85] At that time capitalism took off.

Originally, *usura* simply designated interest, independently of its rate. Today, 'usury' means charging an abusive amount of interest on a loan. But usury is also the procedure that allows the borrower to be imprisoned by a debt that he can no longer repay, and to be deprived of goods that belong to him, but which he has given as collateral for the loan. This is exactly what we see today on a global scale.

Credit allows people to consume future wealth in the present moment. It is based on the utilisation of a virtual sum which is realised by attributing a price to it, the interest. It causes people to lose sight of the elementary principle that one should limit one's expenses to the limits of one's resources, since one cannot live forever beyond one's means. The rapid growth of financial capitalism has favoured this practice: on some days the markets trade the equivalent of ten times the world's GDP, which shows how disconnected they have become from the real economy. When credit becomes

---

85 In 1789, the revolutionary National Assembly began to seize property, which was termed *biens nationaux*, or being for 'the good of the nation'. Property belonging to the Church, the monarchy, and others who were deemed enemies of the Revolution were targeted in this way.—Ed.

a centrepiece of the financial system, one enters into a vicious circle where the discontinuation of credit can cause a widespread collapse of the banking system. The banks have managed to make states come to their rescue again and again by utilising the threat of such a chaotic scenario.

Widely available credit was one of the primary means of expanding capitalism and instituting the consumer society after the Second World War. By going massively into debt, European and American households contributed, to the prosperity of the period of the 'Thirty Glorious Years' between 1948 and 1973. Things changed when mortgage credit got the better of the other forms of credit. 'The mechanism of recourse to a mortgage as a real security of borrowings represents infinitely more than a convenient technique to guarantee the amounts loaned', recalls Jean-Luc Gréau, 'for it upsets the logical framework of allocation, evaluation, and holding of the credits granted. ... Measured risk gives place to a gamble that one takes on the option that one will have, in the case of the debtor's default, of activating the mortgage and seizing the property to resell it under acceptable conditions.' It is this manipulation of mortgages transformed into financial instruments, combined with the multiplication of defaults of payment of borrowers incapable of repaying their debts, which led to the crisis in the autumn of 2008. The same mechanism can be observed today in the public debt crisis, but now at the expense of sovereign states.

We are witnessing a great return of the system of usury. What Keynes called the 'rule of creditors' corresponds to the modern definition of usury. The usurious procedures are found in the manner in which the financial markets and the banks can help themselves to the real assets of indebted states by seizing their assets by way of interest on a debt whose principal constitutes a mountain of virtual money which can never be repaid. Shareholders and creditors are the Shylocks of our time.

But it is the same with debt as with material growth: neither the one nor the other can be prolonged indefinitely. 'Europe committed to finance,' writes Frédéric Lordon, 'is on the point of perishing by finance.' That is what we ourselves wrote a long time ago: the financial system will perish by finance.

Public Debt: How States Have Become Prisoners of Banks

'It is by deficits that men lose their freedom'

—Jacques Rueff

In autumn 2008, an international financial crisis erupted, the epicentre of which was in the United States. One year later, optimistic minds declared that the worst had passed and that the crisis was virtually over. It was not. It is still ongoing and is not close to being over. The worst is not behind, but ahead of us; the consequences will be worse than in 1929. The first phase of the crisis was the result of American households going too deeply into debt. The real economy was made bankrupt as a result of the explosion of private debt, and businesses were hit hard by the collapse of demand, which led to a vast global recession. Today it is states that are over-indebted. The problem of private debt has been followed by the problem of public debt, which today affects most Western countries. How did it come to this?

Let us first take account of the extent of the problem. The public debt in the Eurozone has increased by 26.7% since 2007. Today it represents 80% of the entire GDP of the zone, the public deficits themselves having reached 7% of GDP. But this is only the average level of debt. Since 2011, eight countries have reached debt ratios higher than 80% of their GDP: Hungary and England (80.1%), Germany (83%), France (85%), Portugal (92%), Belgium (97%), Italy (120%), and Greece (160%). These debt levels are in most cases higher than the levels that existed in the majority of developed countries at the end of the First World War or during the recession of the 1930s. Borrowings have contracted at the banks, and especially in the financial markets, thanks to the issuing of bonds.

In France, where the public deficit expected for 2011 is 98.5 billion euros (or 3,200 euros per second throughout the year), the public debt has risen by almost 30% since 2007. Whereas it was only 239 billion euros in 1979, or 21% of the GDP, it exceeded 1,327 billion euros in 2008, 1,489 billion in 2009, and 1,591 billion in 2010. In the first half of 2011 it reached the astronomical figure of 1,681.2 billion euros, or 84.5% of the GDP, with an annual deficit of 7%. These figures do not take into account the commitments that the state has made, and is obligated to pay but which it has not provided for, as for example the pensions of civil servants (commitments evaluated in 2005 of being at least 430 billion euros). In 2011, interest payments on public debt (46.9 billion euros) will represent the second-largest cost in the state budget, second only to education, and far larger than defence and national security spending. Interest payments alone will exceed company tax revenues. In 2012, the interests to be paid will rise to 48.8 billion euros. The issue of long-term debts also represents a direct cost imposed on future generations: in 2011, debts of around 45 billion euros, which will be due between 2040 and 2060, were incurred. Moreover, the debt problem impinges on national sovereignty: in December 2010, 67.7% of the negotiable state debt was held by non-residents.

To the national debt is added the local debt. Since a few years ago, banks have pounced on local authorities in order to make them indebted through an entire series of toxic loans. On 13 July 2011, a report of the Court of Auditors confessed that there are simply no public statistics regarding the structure of the local debt in France. This report, which runs to more than 200 pages, nevertheless estimates that the indebtedness of local authorities (apart from health care institutions) has risen from 116.1 billion euros to 163.3 billion euros in 2010, or an average increase of 41%. (30% for the communes, 63% for the departments, and 80% for the regions).

But the public debt is only one aspect of the total debt, the latter also including the debts of businesses and households. If one takes into consideration all these elements, one arrives at an overall debt of 199.5% of GDP for France in 2010, 202.7% for Germany, 221.1% for Italy, 255% for the UK, 269% for Spain, and 240% for the United States!

The idea that is currently propagated is that the public debts are the results of excess spending by irresponsible governments. That states have not always acted with good sense certainly seems to support that theory, but the root cause of the problem is found elsewhere.

The immediate cause of the growing public debts is connected to the plans to save private banks that a number of governments decided on in 2008 and 2009. The banks have pressed states into rescuing them by stressing the sensitive position that they occupy in the general structure of the capitalist system. To bail out the threatened banks and insurance companies the states, taken hostage, had to borrow on the markets, which increased their debt to unbearable levels. Astronomic amounts (800 billion dollars in the United States, 117 billion pounds in Great Britain) have been expended to prevent the banks from collapsing, which has burdened the public finances to the same extent. In total, the four principal international central banks (the Federal Reserve, the European Central Bank, the Bank of Japan, and the Bank of England) have injected 5000 billion dollars into the world economy between 2008 and 2010. That is the largest transfer of wealth in history from the public sector to the private sector! The banks, when they were repaid, did not contribute to the stock prices. By getting into massive debt to save the banks, the states allowed the banks to immediately resume the same activities that had previously led to their being put at risk. But they have of their own accord placed themselves under the threat of the markets and the credit rating agencies.

Another cause is clearly the economic recession induced by the crisis, which has diminished the revenues of many states and forced them to resort to even more borrowing. But the most distant cause lies in the policies of deregulation and fiscal reform (reduction of taxes on profits paid by private companies, in particular the biggest businesses, and tax breaks for the richest part of the population) which was adopted long before 2008, in the era of Reagan and Thatcher.

The increasing influence of financial lobbies on politicians has led to the progressive deregulation of financial markets, provoking an explosion of speculative gains, draining capital that was previously employed in the productive sector of the economy. For its part, free trade has favoured unfair competition from countries that combine minimal wages with high productivity. Deregulation, obeying the logic of the globalised market as well as the demands of the World Trade Organization, had already led in 1999 to the elimination of all significant customs barriers and the de facto abolition of the so-called 'community advantage' in Europe. The speed with which capital engaged in financial speculation can enter or leave particular economies has increased the volatility of share prices and aggravated the consequences of the crisis.

The consequences are well-known: more outsourcing to other countries, deindustrialisation, lower salaries, decreased job security, and rising unemployment. To that is added the transfers of capital to other countries: in France between 2000 and 2008, 388 billion euros, or an average of 48.5 billion euros per year (which corresponded in 2008 to 2.5% of the GDP), was moved abroad. The only effect of the wave of deregulation which began in the early 1980s has in fact been to further enrich the wealthiest part of the population, while the middle and working classes have seen their incomes stagnate or decline. Income gaps are growing everywhere, unemployment is spreading, and gains in productivity are not accompanied by increases in salaries. Today, unemployment has reached 12% in Portugal, 14% in Ireland, 16% in Greece, and 21% in Spain. Globally, the share of the financial profits increased, whose accumulation of surplus value moved from 10% in the 1950s to more than 40% today.

In spite of the crisis, the new financial oligarchy's stranglehold on the international economy has not stopped reinforcing itself. The profits of the same banks which besieged governments with demands that they be saved from bankruptcy in 2008 bear witness to this. In 2009, after the financial shock of the previous year, the stock values of the six largest American banks (Bank of America, JP Morgan, Citigroup, Wells Fargo, Goldman Sachs, and Morgan Stanley) represented more than 60% of the national GNP while in 1995 they represented only 20%![86] Also in the United States, a recent report by Northeastern University shows that 88% of the real national revenue served to increase the profits of businesses in 2010, while salaries gained from it an increase (if one may call it that) of only a little more than 1%. Never before in American history have the workers received such a small share of the increase in surplus value. One could speak here of a reproletarisation of productive capital by finance capital.

The effects of the concentration of capital in the hands of a small number of financiers have been studied by Paul Jorion. He shows how the multiplication of speculative products has led to the institution of a casino economy which has systematically favoured speculators at the expense of consumers and, sometimes, also at the expense of producers.[87] At the same time, the collusion between the financial markets and organised crime is

---

86   Cf. *PBS+Global Research*, 16 April 2010. In the first quarter of 2010, 80% of 10 billion euros of investment transaction revenues earned by the well-known bank Goldman Sachs resulted from operations effected in its own name, and not in the name of its clients—which however did not prevent it from being subjected to a derisory rate of taxation which led *Newsweek* to speak of the 'moral failure of Goldman Sachs'. Cf. also 'The Moral Failure of Goldman Sachs', *Courrier international*, 6 May 2010. In the beginning of June 2011, Goldman Sachs was the object of a request for information by the Manhattan prosecutor to evaluate its implication in the real estate crisis of 2007. The bank had at that time betted on the collapse of the real estate market even while continuing to sell doctored 'subprimes'. Henry Paulson, appointed Secretary of the Treasury in 2006 by George W Bush, is a former president of Goldman Sachs. The former European Commissioner Mario Monti has been one of its advisors since 2005, which was equally the case with the former President of the European Commission, Romano Prodi. The bank is very generous with those who serve it. Its five principal directors received almost 70 billion dollars in salaries and bonuses in 2010. Its executive director, Lloyd Blankfein, received 14.6 billion dollars.

87   Paul Jorion, *Le capitalisme à l'agonie* (Paris: Fayard, 2011). The author describes in particular the practice of 'day-trading', which designates the cumulative action of a great number of participants in the financial markets who watch the movements of the big financiers to follow in their wake, in this way transforming certain transactions into a tidal wave which completely falsifies the valuation of securities.

highlighted every day. 'The world of finance is eaten away by powerful and discreet criminal forces, but it denies it strongly and even spends fortunes to prevent its coming to light', writes the criminologist Xavier Raufer, who adds: 'Through international deregulation, then the crisis, the illicit economy (grey or black) which constituted some 7% of the gross international product around 1980, unquestionably represented 15% of it in 2009 (or the equivalent of the GNP of Australia).[88]

Another particularly disquieting consequence is the deindustrialisation provoked by the disconnection between the real economy and the financial economy and the explosion of speculative gains which results from it. Among the member countries of the Organisation for Economic Co-operation and Development (OECD),[89] some 17 million industrial jobs have been lost in just two years, of which 10 million were in the manufacturing sectors. If one adds to that figure the 13 or 14 million jobs eliminated in the service sector, one realises the seriousness of this development. The industrial recession, sometimes coyly renamed 'tertiarisation',[90] also affects the United States, which has no more than 11.6 million industrial jobs today, as compared to 19.5 million in 1979 — a 40% decrease in a period when the population continued to increase. Only certain industrialised countries resist this trend — primarily Germany — and certain sectors like the defence industries.

The greatest international power, the United States, has been hit hard. During all the last decade it has been able to serve as an engine for international consumption only by dispensing much more than its national revenue allowed it, which was one of the causes of the deficit that it registered in its balance of current payments. It has, in other words, consumed much more than it has produced (the share of consumption of its GDP is ap-

---

88 *Sécurité globale*, Summer 2011, p. 59.

89 The OECD was launched in 1961 following the Treaty of Rome, which established the European Economic Community with the intention of stimulating international trade and economic growth.—Ed.

90 The shift from industries which produce goods domestically to those industries and services which rely on goods produced abroad.—Ed.

proximately 70%, which is much higher than in most European countries). The result is an enormous debt and record deficits. At the present time, any public expense incurred in the United States is financed by borrowing up to 42% of its cost! On 16 May 2011, the American debt exceeded the so-called 'debt ceiling', reaching 14,294 billion dollars and placing the United States on the verge of having to default on its payments. The political compromise reached *in extremis* on 1 August 2011 between the Republicans and the Democrats raised the debt ceiling, but the deadline has only been postponed. Moreover, the accord only bears on the debt of the federal state and on the capacity of the Treasury to repay the borrowers by calling for more money to be printed, when domestic finances are just as much threatened. President Obama had to commit himself to a plan for drastically reducing the public debt, which had to be effected by cuts imposed, not on the military budget — with soldiers engaged on three fronts (Iraq, Afghanistan, and Libya), it is more gigantic than ever — but on public services and social programmes. These decisions, however, have not prevented credit rating agencies from downgrading the United States for the first time in history, which provoked a sharp decline on the stock exchanges.

The United States, which Vladimir Putin publicly reproached on 2 August 2011 not only for living above its means but also for living as 'parasites on the international economy', again finds itself in a catastrophic situation, both at the level of the federal government and of the federal states, of which 46 (among them California) are either officially bankrupt or in great difficulties. For three years their budgetary deficits have been in the range of 9% to 11% of GDP. Their deficit of the balance of current payments has reached the record level of 400 billion dollars a year. Unemployment is approximately 10%, a figure rarely seen on the other side of the Atlantic.

The US has become the principal debtor of the globe, with more than 3,000 billion dollars in debts owed to the rest of the world (primarily to China). And as its creditors are increasingly averse to holding the debt long-term, it has to borrow shorter-term to finance its deficits, which renders it more vulnerable to the ongoing crisis. Because of this, the confidence in the dollar is melting like snow in the Sun. Since the end of 2010, China has been discreetly decreasing its holdings of American securities. The American Treasury Bonds find increasingly fewer buyers and it is the Federal Reserve itself that buys almost the totality of the bonds issued. In other words, the value of the dollar is only maintained through purchases made by its own issuers! But in the case of a sudden fall of the dollar, China and its other creditors will certainly not accept to see their own share of dollars collapse. The question is what they will demand in return, economically or politically. Perhaps we will see America's abandonment of the defence of Taiwan?

Since two years ago, the financial war conducted by speculators and institutional investors against states is in full swing. The attacks on the financial markets take the form of a direct or indirect rise in interest rates that the countries must pay in order to borrow. The indicators provided by the rating agencies determine the targets and the strategies to be adopted.

The three principal rating agencies — together they represent 95% of the sector — are Standard and Poor's, Fitch Ratings, and Moody's. It is to be noted that it is only recently that they have been authorised to evaluate the financial health, not only of banks and private companies, but also of states. They immediately began to delist the solvency of state borrowings. The drastic series of downgradings of financial rankings that followed their decision to downgrade the credit rating of the United States in August 2011 suffices to show the influence that they exercise. The problem is that their independence can be called into question, since they are financed by the same establishments whose solvency they evaluate: namely, the very banks which pay them to evaluate their products.

A large part of the European public debts are held by banks today, and they have not stopped buying government bonds since 2008 and apparently do not worry unduly about the fragility of public finances, which have been compounded by the recession and the crisis. These purchases of public debt have been financed by money that the banks have borrowed from the European Central Bank (ECB) at nearly zero interest. In other words, the banks have lent to the states, at various interest rates, sums that they themselves have borrowed for almost nothing. But why cannot the states themselves obtain the sums in question directly from the ECB? Quite simply: because they are forbidden to do so!

It was on 3 January 1973 that the French government, in accordance with the proposal of Valéry Giscard d'Estaing, then Finance Minister, adopted a law reforming the statutes of the Bank of France, decreeing that 'the public treasury cannot be the presenter of its own discounted Bank of France bills of exchange' (Article 25). This means that the Bank of France was henceforth prohibited from granting loans to the state, the latter being instead obliged to borrow on the financial markets at interest rates that these are prepared to accept. The private banks, however, can continue to borrow from the ECB at a ridiculously low rate (less than 1%) to lend to the states at a rate varying between 3.5% and 7%. This measure was later standardised throughout Europe by the Maastricht Treaty (Article 104) and the Lisbon Treaty (Article 123). The European states can thus no longer borrow from their central banks. This was a critical turning point, the consequences of which are only becoming clear today. As Léon Camus wrote, the decision taken in 1973 came down to saying that 'the state abandons its right to "mint coins" and transfers this sovereign faculty to the private sector, of which it becomes the voluntary debtor'.

Better still: in autumn 2010, the European Union also accepted that its bonds supported by the new European Financial Stability Facility (EFSF) should no longer be considered prioritised debts, which means that the European states will no longer receive payment before private creditors. The bailing out of banks is henceforth considered more important than safeguarding taxpayers' money!

The most indebted countries (Greece, Ireland, Portugal, etc.) can only receive short-term loans (generally three or six months) on the financial markets. If they wished to borrow money for five or six years, they would have to accept interest rates between 14% and 17%, which would be unbearable for them. The only organisations that are willing to loan to them long-term at lower rates are the International Monetary Fund (IMF), the European Commission, and the European Central Bank (ECB), which have accepted interest rates at 3.5% or 4% but in return demand drastic austerity measures whose principal victims are the working classes. Such measures diminish economic activity, which further erodes the ability of the states subjected to them to repay their debts.

Nevertheless, the financial markets assure us that austerity will bring about confidence and that confidence will generate growth. It is obvious that the reverse is true, since austerity has as its immediate consequence a decrease in incomes, which automatically leads to deflationary pressure on purchasing power, and thus on demand, which can only curb growth and diminish the solvency of states. The austerity plans in reality fall within the 'shock doctrine' that Naomi Klein has described.[91] In France, for example, if it does not manage to 'restore confidence', the French government will have no other choice but to raise taxes (perhaps also the VAT), without the extra income translating into any improvement in public services, since it will have to be used to repay debts. The public services will, on the contrary, be adversely affected since dramatic cuts in the social services and health services are being discussed, after the extension of the retirement age.

The same pattern is found in all countries. In the final analysis, it is always a question of saving the states only to avoid a new collapse of international finance. That is the reason why the demands of the creditors have systematically been taking precedence over those of the citizens. Only two possibilities then remain: either the austerity measures become so severe that they end in a general revolt, or debts reach the point that repayment becomes impossible and bankruptcy cannot be avoided. The demands for

---

91 In her book, *The Shock Doctrine: The Rise of Disaster Capitalism*, Klein theorises that part of the reason that liberal economics have risen to such prominence in recent decades is that governments exploit crises in order to push through liberal economic policies while their populations are distracted by other problems.—Ed.

PUBLIC DEBT: HOW STATES HAVE BECOME PRISONERS OF BANKS

austerity measures have already shown themselves to be ineffective in Latin America and Asia. It will not work better in Europe.

Public opinion knows this. Already 'the indices of household confidence are lower than the historical average in all of the major Western countries, without exception'.[92] An IFOP[93] survey published in June 2011 by economists united under the banner of the 'Manifesto for a Debate on Free Trade' has revealed that a vast majority of the French are henceforth favourable to protectionism and perfectly aware of the 'harmful effects of globalisation'. More than 70% of them believe that the opening of borders has negative consequences for employment (84%), the level of salaries (78%), and public deficits (73%). Approximately 65% declare themselves openly in favour of raising customs taxes, regardless of what political camp they belong to (69% of those on the Left, 72% of those on the Right, 69% of those in the Front National, and 75% of those in the UMP!).[94]

The Greek affair is clearly an example of what awaits the rest of Europe.

In the past, it appeared that the euro offered the Greeks the godsend of a stable currency and almost unlimited credit, which saved them from having to correct the grave problems in their economy. They were hypnotised by a deceptive growth solely stimulated by borrowing. But the euro revealed itself very quickly to be a trap: as the Greeks produce few products with large added value, they found it difficult to export much. And as they no longer had a national currency that they could devalue, it was quite naturally borrowing and employment that became the principal variables of adjustment.

Today the amount of public debt in Greece is at least 350 billion euros, which corresponds to more than 160% of its GDP, with a deficit in the balance of current transactions close to 10%. In addition, there are the debts of businesses and households and, not to forget, the capital flight caused to a

---

92 Jean-Luc Gréau, 'Le rétablissement ou la rechute?', *Le Débat*, September–October 2010, p. 41.

93 Institut français d'opinion publique (French Institute of Public Opinion).—Ed.

94 Union pour un mouvement populaire (Union for a Popular Movement), centre-Right and one of France's two major political parties.

large extent by the loss of confidence in the Greek banks. Dmitri Kousselas, Secretary of State in the Greek Ministry of Finance, estimates the amount of Greek funds that have recently been transferred to Switzerland at being 280 billion euros, or 120% of the GDP!

No longer being able to finance themselves long-term on the financial markets on account of their situation, the Greeks turned to the IMF and the European Union. A first call for help in April 2010 ended in a 'rescue package' of 110 billion euros over three years: 80 billion allocated directly by the states of the Eurozone or through the European mechanisms, the contribution of each country being calculated on the basis of its participation in the capital of the ECB — or, for France, 16.8 billion euros (21%), the equivalent of a third of the income tax — and 30 billion allocated by the IMF. But it quickly became clear that this sum would not be enough. In July 2011, at the Brussels summit, a new rescue plan arranged for an additional grant of 109 billion euros to Greece, 79 billion coming from the IMF and the European Financial Stability Facility (EFSF) created some months earlier, with a further 30 billion called to result from a privatisation plan.

In this affair, the German and French banks are the most exposed. At the end of 2010, French banks already owned 15 billion euros of Greek public debt (4.5 billion for the BNP Paribas, 2.5 billion for the Société générale, 2 billion for Groupama, etc.). The exposure of the Crédit agricole goes through its Greek affiliate Emporiki, the sixth-largest bank in the country, which alone owns 21.1 billion euros of Greek debt. Rescuing Greece thus amounts to rescuing the French banks (which explains why the Moody's agency has already placed three French banks under 'negative surveillance' due to their exposure to Greek risk). France thus borrows money from banks which will be given to Greece to repay banks! The situation is surreal. But, at the same time, it is easy to understand the consequences that a definitive bankruptcy of the state of Greece would entail for French financial institutions. A Greek default of payments could spread to other countries, putting the whole European banking system at risk of bankruptcy.

While Germany proposed that the 'pain should be shared' (by means of a so-called 'haircut') between Greece's public and private creditors so that the European taxpayers would not be the only ones to assume the burden of the Greek debt, at the Brussels summit the rescue of the Greek economy was conceived in a way that would spare the big banks as much as possible. Immediately exonerated of the bank tax which could have hit them, they were given three options: to sell their bonds at market price to the EFSF, to exchange them against 30-year bonds on conditions which were not specified, or quite simply to renew their bonds as they became due (in the last two cases, the debt would not be reduced but repaid at a later stage). Equal care was taken not to touch the prerogatives of the ECB, which could have been extended to partially redeem the debt.[95] Ultimately, it was the taxpayers who would pay for Greece. The banks, supported by the central banks, the financial markets, and the rating agencies, are more than ever in a position of strength. And, consequently, in a good position to raise the stakes. This has allowed them to demand at Brussels, at the same time as they sought to dismantle the prudential regulations adopted within the framework of Basel III, the maximum conceivable amount of interest and guarantees as the price of their future participation. In 2008, governments indebted themselves in order to rescue the banks. In 2011, by inventing new institutions supposed to come to the aid of the states, they rescued them a second time.

---

95 The independence of the ECB, which had from the start opposed all readjustment of the Greek debt susceptible to being related to a 'credit event', however, poses a problem. We know that its new director, Mario Draghi, who succeeded Jean-Claude Trichet in June 2011, occupied the post of governor of the Bank of Italy before that. This individual is very controversial. As the head of the Italian treasury, he played an important role in the large privatisations decided on in Italy at the time of the move to the euro. Above all, from 2002 to 2005, he was international Vice President for Europe of the American bank Goldman Sachs, an institution directly implicated in the Greek crisis, since in 2001 it helped Greece conceal the extent of the debt (in exchange for a fee of 300 million dollars!). Obviously it is hard to believe that he will be able to oppose tomorrow what he promoted yesterday.

At the same time as aid has been given to Greece, European institutions and the IMF have demanded that Greece implement austerity plans and drastic cuts in the form of unprecedented waves of privatisation in public services, for example of airports and ports (the port of Piraeus is already under Chinese control) and including defence industries, widespread deregulation, reduction of the number of civil servants, reductions in salaries, fiscal reforms for which the middle and working classes will pay the price, drastic cuts in social programmes, pensions and health budgets, etc., all measures which would result in a lowering of purchasing power by almost 40% — a reduction unlike any that a nation has ever had to suffer in peacetime. Under these conditions, it will be easy for foreign groups to buy up the country's resources at a low price and to reinvest their profits elsewhere. It is already clear that the 'rescue plans' applied to Greece would cause the share of the Greek debt held by foreigners to increase to 64%, compared with 26% in 2010. At the moment, attempts are made to bring about an auctioning off of the assets of the country. The German MPs Josef Schlarmann (CDU)[96] and Frank Schäffler (FDP)[97] recently cynically declared: 'The Greeks only have to sell their islands and their monuments to repay us'!

In reality, the deadlines are only being postponed, since none of these measures can eliminate the main causes of Greece's bankruptcy. Each new loan to Greece results in a contraction of economic activity, compounding the problem instead of solving it. The financial 'aid' granted to Greece has this in common with the military 'aid' given to Afghanistan: it only grants a temporary respite. Add to this the inflation differential of the past, the chronic overvaluation of the euro, the aggravation of deficits and the increase in foreign debts that result from it, can only result in a postponement of the problem for a short while, the same causes automatically generating the same effects. There is every chance that Greece will soon have

---

[96] Christlich Demokratische Union Deutschlands, or the Christian Democratic Union of Germany.—Ed.

[97] Freie Demokratische Partei, or Free Democratic Party.—Ed.

to choose between leaving the euro or suffering large-scale impoverishment of its population.

The consequences of the Greek crisis are so much more remarkable in that Greece represents only 2.5% of the GDP of the Eurozone. Its economy is only one-sixth the size of Italy's. What will happen when it is time to rescue countries of a much greater size? Matters could proceed very rapidly. Let us not forget that it was only a short while ago that countries like Ireland and Spain, which today are in the first line of fire, were still considered safe borrowers by virtue of their budget surpluses: in 2007, the Irish budget was stable, the deficit of Portugal did not exceed 2.6%, and Spain registered a budget surplus of 2%. Hence the fear that the crisis will prove contagious. What is in the cards today is no longer the situation of Greece or Portugal but the entry of Spain or Italy, or even France and Great Britain, into the storm zone. Philippe Dessertine, director of the Institute of High Finance and professor at Paris-X, believes that France 'is the next country on the list': 'The question is not so much if we will be affected', he says, 'but rather when.'

According to the OECD, in order for the public debt of France to return to a level of 60% of the GDP, public administrations must realise a budgeted surplus for at least ten years. The last surplus budget dates from 1974! To improve the situation, in principle there exists only two possibilities: to increase the resources of the state or to decrease public spending. Raising taxes is difficult to envisage in a country which is already the most heavily taxed in the world among developed countries. As for public spending, which represent 56.2% of the GDP in France, far more than Germany (46.6%) or even Spain (45%), no one has a clear idea of how to reduce expenses to the extent that would be necessary.

When public debt becomes unbearable (that is to say, when debt ratios exceed 35% of the GNP), countries no longer have the choice between letting inflation increase (this is what happened in Germany under the Weimar Republic) or defaulting on payments. The establishment of the euro has made it impossible for a country to issue more of its currency. History shows that, once a certain threshold has been passed, a large public debt almost inevitably leads to bankruptcy. It is difficult to see, taking into consideration the damage caused by the Greek affair alone, how the European institutions could deal with a series of sovereign debt crises, successive or simultaneous, of much greater proportions. 'In the present European reality', writes Frédéric Lordon, 'the more countries that need rescuing, the fewer rescuers are left, and the members of the latter category increasingly tend to join the former', which is the same as saying that 'the splendid mechanisms of the capital markets converge with a rare elegance with the worst organisation in rendering the debt crisis insoluble that they themselves have created'.[98]

One thing is certain: a general policy of austerity is on the way in Europe, whose principal victims will be the working classes and the middle classes, with all the risks inherent in such a situation. As new countries find themselves in a state of bankruptcy, the citizens of the entire European Union will be asked to pay the bill. Now, let us say clearly: no country today is capable of stopping its debt from rising in terms of its share of the GDP, and none is able to repay the principal of its debt. In spite of all delay tactics, a full-scale explosion seems inevitable within a couple of years. Like many others, Jean-Luc Gréau believes that the system will not be able to find a new equilibrium on its own.[99] The economist Philippe Dessertine goes so far as to predict a 'profound geopolitical crisis which could end in a world war'.[100] Such words could seem alarmist. But the capitalist system has never shied before the possibility of war, when that was the only way to protect its interests. What would happen if the greatest world power, the United States, was forced to default on its payments? In Europe, the present status

---

98 'La pompe à phynance,' blog of *Le Monde diplomatique*, 2 December 2010.
99 *Art. cit.*
100 *Le Point*, 13 July 2011.

quo leads, because of its cumulative effects, directly into a depression of a magnitude never seen before.

The politicians have surrendered control of finance to the markets. The markets maintain for their part that financial affairs are too serious to be left to the whims of politicians. We have seen the result: cascading bankruptcies, an international financial crisis, increasing private and public debt. Private finance seems to have already precipitated the largest crisis in the history of capitalism. How can we get out of this predicament?

The solutions are, unfortunately, only theoretical. On a purely technical level, it would be perfectly possible to force the banks to write off a series of items on their balance sheets that correspond to so many doubtful or illegitimate loans. One could also impose a new banking discipline which would prohibit commercial banks from merging with deposit banks. At the time of the New Deal, Roosevelt had already adopted the Glass-Steagall Act, which forced the banking sector to split up into commercial and investment banks on the one hand, and savings and deposit banks on the other. (This arrangement was abolished by the Clinton administration.) One could envision fiscal policies permitting better control of the movements of short-term capital, the obligation of the ECB to partially finance the repayment of national debts, as well as making a clear distinction between 'productive' and 'speculative' interest rates. The law of 1973 forbidding the Bank of France to buy treasury bonds should obviously be abolished. A more radical measure would be the nationalisation, pure and simple and without compensation, of the banking sector and other key sectors of the economy. Frédéric Lordon, who supported the nationalisation of the banking system and the 'communalisation' of credit thereby makes so many preambles to the ultimate transformation of credit into a truly socialist system. But that will not happen anytime soon, no country having the least intention of declaring open war on the financial interests, even (and especially) when they have been bled white by those very interests.

To submit the international markets to a new global regulation 'from above' of the Keynesian type is almost impossible. Under present conditions, that would imply the establishment of tribunals capable of imposing penal sanctions — for example, in the case of speculation on a collective asset such as a national currency, or in the case of the exploitation of public debts in order to plunder a country. This remains wishful thinking. The solution is rather to recentre the European Union on itself, by establishing a stronger co-operation around a 'hard core' of some of its members.

As Frédéric Lordon further writes, '"serious" re-regulation is envisaged only at the regional level', that is to say, on spaces geographically limited but also politically closed by a principle of sovereignty, whatever the level of the latter may be. It is only within such limits that restricting measures may be enforceable. Within such a framework, the solution includes not only measures aiming at a political stoppage of the excesses of capital, but also the relocalisation of businesses (supported by fiscal incentives), the realigning of economic production with consumption, localisation, regulation on a regional level, etc., all measures which could be described as being part of a certain form of 'deglobalisation'.[101]

Rejecting widespread deregulation — beginning with capital, goods, and services — would allow us to go further. But that would require, apart from a political will which does not exist today,[102] definitively abandoning the ideological paradigm that is dominant today. 'At the very heart of the capitalist ideology', Raoul Weiss reminds us, 'one finds a deep-rooted rejection of the political unification of spaces united *de facto* by economics.'[103] Since the time of Adam Smith, David Hume, and Bernard Mandeville, then Ricardo, the theory of 'free markets' has been based on states aban-

---

101 Unfortunately, certain champions of 'another globalisation', for whom deglobalisation is only a synonym for 'withdrawal into national self-interest', do not wish to see this. See the excellent response recently made to them by Frédéric Lordon, who emphasises that the expression 'liberal globalisation' is only a tautology and that those who wish for the first element without having the second expose themselves to serious disappointments ('Qui a peur de la démondialisation?', blog of *Le Monde diplomatique*, 13 June 2011).

102 Cf. Henry A. Giroux, *Zombie Politics and Culture in the Age of Casino Capitalism* (New York: Peter Lang, 2010).

103 'Le gauchisme, garant de la *transitio imperiorum* oligarchique', *La Pensée libre* website, June 2011.

doning their national sovereignty. To break that paradigm would be the equivalent of breaking with all the liberal dogmas of the 'invisible hand', the 'freedom of the markets', the 'rational' anticipations, the 'fundamental' role of 'spontaneous' competition, the benefits of 'flexibility' and of free trade, the theory of the 'automatic balance' of international commerce, and so on. It would be to show that all these theories are based, not on 'natural laws', but on unrealistic hypotheses (perfect and complete information available to the economic actors,[104] spontaneous adjustment of supply and demand, etc.), making them scientifically untenable.

Challenging 'high finance' or the international financial markets is pointless as long as it is done, as one often sees on the Right, in order to simultaneously favour petty national, industrial, and 'non-financial' capitalisms that would not stop from being systems which exploit human labour when their activities are reframed within a national context. It does not become more attractive if, as one often sees on the Left, it is done to oppose to the movements of liberal capital a simple rhetoric of the 'citizen', most often separated from the people, based on a moralistic 'indignation', compassionate reformism, and solidarity with the 'excluded' (a term borrowed from 'humanitarian' vocabulary in order not to have to speak of the workers or of the proletariat).

It is certainly not by limiting oneself to being 'indignant', as it is fashionable to be today, that one will manage to bring about change. Indignation that does not result in concrete action is only a comfortable way of relieving one's conscience. Only the resolute intervention of the working and middle classes in the battle can give to the 'indignation' that the practices of the capitalist system arouse, or to the widespread discontentment with the banks, the social basis that they still lack — so that the action to be conducted is situated below or beyond the limits of bourgeois legality.

---

104 Adam Smith (1723–1790) was a Scottish economist who helped to lay the foundation for modern-day capitalism. He advanced the idea that individual self-interest was ultimately good for all of society.—Ed.

The Euro Should Be Made a Common Currency

The decision to give Europe a single currency was originally made by François Mitterrand and Helmut Kohl, during the European summit in Rome in December 1990. But it was only on 1 January 1999 that the euro officially came into force, and it was only from 1 January 2002 that notes and coins in euros replaced many of the national currencies in Europe. The euro is thus only ten years old, and it is already being questioned, since the crisis of the euro is at the centre of the financial turmoil in Europe.

But there is no reason to confuse the European Union with the present single currency. The euro and Europe are not synonymous. That is already proven by the fact that certain countries of the European Union (Denmark, Sweden, the United Kingdom) never entered the Eurozone. As Mark Weisbrot wrote in *The Guardian*, 'There is no reason that the European project cannot proceed, and the European Union prosper, without the euro.'[105]

The establishment of the euro would have been an excellent thing if it had respected two conditions: that the level of the single currency should not be pegged on the old deutschmark, and that its establishment must be accompanied by a system of commercial protection at the borders. None of these conditions was fulfilled. Instead of ensuring community protection, it was the card of integral free trade that was played. In 1994, one

---

105 'Why the euro is not worth saving', *The Guardian*, 11 July 2011.

witnessed the dismantlement of the common external tariff which, up to then, had partially protected Europe from competition, in social dumping conditions, from low income countries. The chronic overvaluation of the euro then highlighted the imbalances. At the same time, a single currency was tacked onto economies that were divergent in every respect. The crisis was from that time inevitable.

The basic problem of the euro flows from the obvious fact that there cannot be a single currency uniting countries of structurally divergent economies. One cannot apply the same monetary policy, that is to say, the same exchange rates and the same rates of interest to economies of different structures and levels. Such a zone is inevitably transformed into a zone of transfers, the richest having to pay for the poorest in order to compensate for their economic weakness. This is what the Greek crisis has demonstrated.

Philippe Séguin[106] said it already on 5 May 1992 on the platform of the National Assembly: 'As soon as there is only a single currency in a given territory, the gaps in standard of living between the regions that constitute it quickly become unbearable. And, in the case of an economic crisis, it is unemployment that is imposed as the only variable of adjustment.' Two years later, Jimmy Goldsmith[107] affirmed in a prophetic manner: 'The project of a single currency ... would mean that a country like Greece would not be able to adjust its currency in relation to that of the Netherlands, for example. We know the result of that: either the transfer of subsidies to countries in difficulty or the transfer of unemployed people from this country to more prosperous ones.'[108] These observations join the many warnings given a long time ago by Maurice Allais.[109]

---

106 Philippe Séguin (1943–2010) was a deputy in the National Assembly in 1992, later becoming its President from 1993 until 1997, and then serving as President of the Court of Financial Auditors from 2004 until his death. In 1992 he was one of the leading opponents of the Maastricht Treaty.—Ed.

107 Jimmy Goldsmith (1933–1997) was an Anglo-French billionaire who was elected as a Member of the European Parliament from France in 1994, where he established the eurosceptic Europe of Nations group.—Ed.

108 Jimmy Goldsmith, *Le piège* (Paris: Fixot, 1994).

109 Maurice Allais, *La crise mondiale d'aujourd'hui* (Paris: Clément Juglar, 1999).

The euro has thus been adopted in countries strongly divergent from the economic point of view, a situation that the Maastricht 'criteria' have not corrected in any way. Better still, the more economic integration was deepened, the more this divergence has grown. As for the convergence of the short-term interest rates, it has led to a greater divergence of fiscal policies. The application of a single interest rate to economies endowed with a different inflation rate has been one of the major sources of the inflation of debt in countries like Greece, Spain, or Portugal. 'The euro has been to the sovereign debts what the free sale of firearms is to the considerable number of homicides in the United States: a spur to crime', remarked Nicolas Dupont-Aignan.[110]

Traditionally, a state which becomes indebted in its external trade has the possibility to redress the situation by devaluing its national currency (the price of its exports will be reduced for buyers in proportion to the rates of devaluation). But 'competitive devaluations' are evidently no longer possible with the euro. Besides, the euro has been overvalued for years (today it is worth around 1.4 dollars, compared to 1 dollar at the time it was instituted). This overvaluation is the result of the game in the markets. A strong currency reassures the eventual lenders of the repayment capacities of those whom they finance, which allows them to not demand interest rates that are too high. Conversely, a weak currency pushes them to increase their interest rates.

Having ensured that the value of the euro would be aligned with the old deutschmark from the start, the Germans (along with Austria and the Netherlands) are the only ones to have really benefited from the euro. In 2009, Germany accumulated 140 billion euros as surplus of its commercial balance, essentially to the detriment of its Eurozone partners and the members of the European Union that do not belong to this zone (82.6 and 3.2 billion euros, respectively). The high cost of the euro is, in turn, at the source of the external deficits of all the countries in the south of Europe.

---

110 Nicolas Dupont-Aignan (b. 1961) is a French Gaullist politician.—Ed

Their exports diminishing by virtue of the level of the euro, and their imports continuing to increase, their external deficits have exploded, resulting in a diminution of productive investment and the multiplication of delocalisations.

With the Greek affair, we have begun to see gigantic financial transfers from the countries of the north to the south in amounts which can only become unbearable very quickly. One cannot, for example, see the Germans — who already had to support the upgrading of the old GDR in the past — accepting to see their imports double or triple in order to come to the rescue of other countries of Europe which have been placed in difficulty. The call to solidarity thus risks not reinforcing Europe but weakening it. 'By wishing to save the euro', thinks Nicolas Dupont-Aignan, 'the blind leaders are in the process of destroying Europe. For Europe has no meaning unless it permits each people to prosper more with the others than they could in isolation.'

The dominant political class chose defeat in advance: to do everything to 'save the euro' without touching the financial system that is in place. Is that even realistic? The American economist Nouriel Roubini has recently predicted the break-up of the Eurozone in the coming five years. He already foresees in 2013 the outbreak of the 'perfect storm'. The end of the euro, according to him, would permit the countries of the south of Europe to restore their competitiveness by means of a massive devaluation of their restored national currencies.[111] This opinion is shared by many other experts, some of whom do not hesitate to advocate a return to these old national currencies.

The major argument that is generally opposed to an eventual exit from the euro is that the countries that would be endangered thereby would instantaneously see their debt increase, since it would continue to be drawn in euros. One may reply that, on the other hand, these countries could adopt measures capable of favouring the rise of internal demand and the

---

111 *Financial Times*, 14 June 2011.

re-establishment of their competitiveness, which would allow them on the contrary to better deal with their debt. A return to national currencies combined with a strong devaluation — comparable to what happened in the countries of the eastern bloc when they abandoned the rouble after the collapse of the Soviet system — would lower the cost of products for foreign buyers and stimulate exports to the same degree, which would provide a better means of regulating the debt. It has also been noted that every devaluation following a return to national currencies would inevitably result in a price increase of products imported from outside the Eurozone. But this objection is, in fact, quite weak: for France, the imports of goods and services from outside the Eurozone represents only 13% of the GDP.

But the optimal solution would evidently be to proceed to a massive devaluation, nominal and real, of the euro before a return to national currencies, which would permit an exit from it without damages. The lowering of the parity of the euro vis-à-vis the dollar would favour the reduction of external deficits and contribute to make the sovereign debts of countries that have restored their currency more sustainable. In order to avoid an increase in debt, the latter could be converted into a common currency representing the average of the national currencies.

In a text that appeared in *Le Figaro*, co-written by Jacques Sapir and Philippe Villon, the economist Gérard Lafay has thus taken a stand for the transformation of the euro into a simple common currency. It would in fact be perfectly possible to conserve the sole incontestable advantage of the euro — of eventually constituting a reserve currency — by transforming the present single currency into a common currency at a level determined in relation to the euro and the restored national currencies. 'This new system would allow the parities between the different European currencies to be changed once a year in order to ensure a reasonable monetary competitiveness within the European Union for each country, and that even while continuing to have a unified European currency in relation to the other major world currencies' (Nicolas Dupont-Aignan). The common currency establishes a barrier in relation to the rest of the world but does not prohibit the adjustment of the exchange parities between the member countries. Even if the euro maintained itself at its present level in a certain number of countries of the zone, the possibility would still remain of establishing a common currency with certain countries alone, within the framework of a system of fixed but revisable exchanges and a strict control of capital.

This solution is very different from that of the European 'economic government' that some would like to institute to remedy the crisis. Those who argue for this solution consider it in fact as a fiscal federalism.[112] No monetary or fiscal union has ever been able to survive in the absence of a political union. To put an economic government in place before, and in the absence of, a political government would be an aberration.

To leave the euro would not at all be sufficient to free oneself from the dictatorship of the banks and the markets. The return to national currencies is in fact not a panacea. It would not resolve any of the structural problems of companies as they presently exist and would not in any way constitute a break with the system of capital. 'To recover our monetary sovereignty would be meaningless unless it is accompanied by a radical change of our politics', thinks Jacques Sapir very rightly, according to whom an eventual exit from the euro should be prepared 'like a military operation'.[113]

Are some states going to be forced to leave the euro? Do the crackles that can be heard in the Eurozone announce a full-scale explosion? Are we moving in the short term to a terminal crisis? And in the long term to world bankruptcy? The European structure, in any case, is today experiencing a historic crisis such as it has never known since its beginnings in 1957. Europe, where the former nation-states have transformed themselves into so many market-states, is simultaneously on the path to geopolitical

---

112 G Dussouy and B Yvars, of the Université de Bordeaux IV, have thus spoken out for the reactivation of a European federalist project, the only one capable, in their view, of 'reassembling the last living strengths of the continent' ('Bien-être et consolidation de l'État de droit dans l'UE dans le contexte de la globalisation', online text, July 2010).

113 Cf. Jacques Sapir, *La fin de l'euro-libéralisme* (Paris: Seuil, 2010); *La démondialisation* (Paris: Seuil, 2011).

marginalisation, ageing, social destruction, deindustrialisation, and impoverishment. One cannot escape the showdown.

Middle Classes and Working Classes: A Politics of Poverty

'When shit becomes valuable, the poor will be born without assholes.'

—Henry Miller[114]

Crisis? What crisis? The big financial crisis of 2008 only showed the banks and the big companies that, in case of difficulties, the public funds will always be there to bail them out. For the richest, whose stake the state has rescued, the profits never stopped. In the United States, nobody responsible for the failure of real estate credit (the famous 'subprimes') has been sanctioned. The few who have been prosecuted have been acquitted and, thanks to their networks, the 'barons' of Wall Street have already got back on their feet again. Today, as yesterday, the profits of the insurance companies and banking institutions who have owed their survival only to the massive intervention of the public powers continue to soar.

In April 2010, one thus learned that the managers of speculative funds (hedge funds) attained record sums in 2009, the first five having each earned more than a billion dollars. The leader of the class was the American David Tepper of Appaloosa Management's hedge funds, which realised 4 billion dollars — never seen before in this sector — the second on the list being the American financier of Hungarian origin, George Soros, who earned 3.3 billion dollars. In total, the 25 highest-paid leaders of specula-

---

[114] This phrase appeared in Portuguese at the bottom of personalised stationery that Miller used to write letters on.—Ed.

tive funds in the world realised 25.3 billion dollars, or double what they earned in 2008. Which means that, 'on the public funds loaned in the course of the year 2009, either at very low rates or at zero rates, to save the international economic system from total collapse, the managers and owners of the most important hedge funds have realised unprecedented benefits during a crisis which yet continues. They simply took the benefits from the interest and those services that had been acquired through the use of the public money.'[115]

The same thing is true for the biggest French banks. For the first half of 2010, the National Bank of Paris (BNP) registered a net profit of 4.4 billion euros (for a 'turnover' of 13 billion). A document ('Profil financier du CAC 40')[116] published in September 2010 by Ricol Lasteyrie, a company specialising in financial expertise and investment advising, shows that the big businesses of the CAC 40 have, for their part, realised a net profit in 2009 of 46 billion euros, followed by a still higher profit of 42 billion euros in the first half of 2010! The document specifies that these profits result principally from a reduction of costs, the result of the multiplication of precarious work contracts, delocalisations towards countries in which low salaries are paid, and the search for subcontractors abroad.

In total, the very big European and American companies today find themselves in possession of 843 billion dollars (a little more than twice the budget of France) in surplus liquidity, a sum which is going first to serve to increase the amount of dividends paid to the shareholders, and second to realise stock repurchases, mergers, or acquisitions which would allow the companies to increase their size. We thus witness a continuing movement of the concentration of capital gains made by these businesses, this being no longer redistributed to the workers or the households but remaining confined to the top of the system.

---

[115] Claude Karnoouh, 'Obscenitatea etica a capitalismului', *Cultura*, 29 April 2010, p. 1.
[116] Available at piketty.pse.ens.fr/files/RicolLasteyrie_ProfilCAC40_2012.pdf.—Ed.

Between 2000 and 2007 the profits of the businesses of the CAC 40 increased globally by 97% and the dividends that they allowed to be distributed increased by 255% — whereas investment diminished by 23%. In 2007, the directors of the businesses of the CAC 40 each earned, on average, 6.2 billion euros compared to 2.2 billion in 2006.

There is no question of increasing the employers' contributions to finance the pensions, declares the MEDEF.[117] But, at the same time, the big businesses listed on the stock exchange do not hesitate to furnish colossal sums to finance the precious complementary pensions of a certain number of big bosses. It is a question of the famous 'top hat pension plans' offered by management boards to their directors to complete their basic plans, which have as a double characteristic that they amount to millions of euros and are only very slightly taxed. According to the authority of the financial markets, about one hundred directors of listed businesses (CAC 40 and SBF 120)[118] benefit from this very special plan in France. Let us quote some figures: Lindsay Owen-Jones left L'Oréal in 2006 with a 'top hat plan' of 3.4 million euros per year (400 times the minimum old age pension!), Antoine Zacharias left Vinci the same year with 2.2 million euros per year, and Jean-René Fourtou left Aventis in 2002 with 1.6 million euros per year. In total, 24 of the old big business bosses receive close to 30 million euros of 'top hat pension plans' per year. During the ten years that preceded his departure upon retirement, the remuneration of Antoine Zacharias, champion of stock options, rose to a total of 250 million euros.

Let us not forget the indemnities, either: Mark Hurd, who in August 2010 had to resign from his post as CEO of Hewlett-Packard as a result of a sexual harassment inquiry, left with indemnities rising to a total of 28 million dollars.

---

117 'Why would the rich, who have already paid the heaviest taxes in the world [sic], be concerned about the pension of social insurance beneficiaries who are neither their brothers nor their sons nor their cousins', coldly declares the very liberal Philippe Nemo (online interview, *Le temps d'y penser* site, 29 September 2010). (MEDEF is the Movement des Entreprises de France, is the largest employers' organisation in France.—Ed.)

118 The CAC 40 and SBF 120 are French stock market indices.—Ed.

According to the magazine *Capital* (November 2008), the average salaries, including stock options, of the top 50 French bosses represented 310 times the Smic three years ago.[119] If one adds dividends, one arrives at the equivalent of more than 20,000 times the Smic for each of the most fortunate! But it is not always necessary to direct a business to earn a lot of money. Everybody knows the case of Liliane Bettencourt, that charming old lady whose fortune is evaluated at 15 billion euros and who received from the L'Oréal group founded by her father the tidy sum of 280 million euros in dividends in 2009, which did not prevent her, as everybody knows, from also receiving a cheque for 32 million euros of the public treasury as a 'fiscal shield' in 2008.

It is clear that no talent and no ability justifies the receipt of such sums. Henry Ford himself thought that he should not earn more than 40 times the salary of his lowest-paid worker. George Orwell advocated a maximum gap of 1 to 10. In the United States, the salaries of the CEOs of the major corporations have moved from 20 times the average worker's salary in 1980 to ... 531 times in 2000! Which poses, in the eyes of some, the question of knowing if it would not be desirable to establish a maximum income or, at least, to re-establish a true tax increase.[120]

After having questioned 114 international financial institutions, the Boston Consulting Group (BCG) calculated that the 'wealth of the world' — the assets under management — reached 111,500 billion dollars in 2009, or 11.5% more than the preceding year. Europe and the United States remain globally the richest regions in the world, since two-thirds of the world's wealth is concentrated there (37,100 billion dollars for Europe, 351,000 billion for North America), although Asia is also well represented. This international wealth is supposed to continue to increase by 6% from now until 2014.

---

119 Salaire Minimum Interprofessionel de Croissance, the guaranteed minimum growth-indexed wage.—Ed.
120 Cf. Jean Gadrey, *En finir avec les inégalités* (Paris: Mango, 2006).

According to a United Nations report from 2006, 10% of the population of the world controlled 85% of the world's wealth at that time, 2% possessing half of it. The millionaires in dollars represent today only 1% of the world's population but hold close to 40% of the world's wealth. As for the richest of the rich, that is to say, the households that possess more than 5 million dollars, they represent only 0.1% of the world's population, but they arrogated to themselves some 21% of the world's wealth in 2009 (2% more than in 2008). In 2008, the 225 richest people in the world thus disposed of the same financial resources as the 2.5 billion poorest individuals. And the trend is regularly increasing: between 1960 and 1993 the share of the richest 20% of the planet moved from 70% to 85% of the world's GDP, whereas those of the poorest 20% moved from 2.3% to 1.4%, the ratio between their respective percentages moving from 30 to 1 to 78 to 1.[121]

In France, as elsewhere, the GDP has not stopped growing, but this growth has not equally profited all the segments of the population. The returns on capital had already doubled between 1982 and 1995, whereas the percentage of the salaries in the GDP was lowered by 9.1%. From 2000 to 2006 the returns of 'investment capital' (share dividends, returns on bonds, etc.) declared for income tax moved from 14.5 billion to 18.8 billion euros, or a progression of 29.6%. The surplus gains also rose by 68% in four years. This explosion of high incomes has been confirmed for the first time by the INSEE[122] in its 2010 edition of its study on *Les revenus et le patrimoine des ménages*.[123] According to this report, the capital revenues and the 'exceptional' revenues (for example, the sales of stock options) underwent vertiginous increases on the order of 46% and 55% respectively between 2004 and 2007, whence this observation that 'inequalities in France are growing prodigally'.

---

121 Cf. Lant Pritchett, 'Divergence, Big Time', *Journal of Economic Perspectives*, Summer 1997.

122 Institut National de la Statistique et des Études Économiques (the French National Institute for Statistics and Economic Studies)—Ed.

123 *The Incomes and Wealth of Households*—Ed.

One uses the term 'very high incomes' to describe those of people situated in the 1% richest segment of the population.[124] This stratum, which represents around 600,000 individuals in France, corresponds to an average annual income of 100,000 euros. For the wealthiest section of these very rich, or 5,800 persons (0.01% of the population), the income ranges between 680,000 and 13 million euros per year, with an average of 1.27 million euros a year. The INSEE specifies that the number of people whose standard of living exceeds an annual 100,000 euros rose by 28% between 2004 and 2007, whereas it increased by 70% for those who earn more than 500,000 euros. As for the 0.01% richest, in 2007 they earned 40% more than in 2004, or 360,000 additional annual euros, whereas the 90% poorest earned only 9% more, or 1,400 euros. This enrichment is partly due to the increase in work incomes: whereas the rise in these work incomes was 9% in three years for 90% of the population (a rate hardly better than inflation), it reached nearly 30% among the very rich, and nearly 40% among the richest. But work by itself rarely allows for the saving of a fortune. As the economist Laurent Cordonnier has noted, 'salaried work, leaving aside a minority of privileged people who share the dividends of capital without ever risking a cent in business, has never enriched anybody. ... It is indeed rather by making others work that one enriches oneself.'[125] In fact, if the high incomes represent a quarter of work incomes, they also receive two-thirds of the property incomes and four-fifths of the 'exceptional' incomes. The richest 1% themselves receive 5.5% of work incomes, 32.4% of property incomes, and almost half of the exceptional incomes.

To sum up, the richer one is, the more chances one has to become even richer. One knew it already from the works of the economists Thomas Piketty and Camille Landais of the École d'économie de Paris, which had

---

[124] To compare living standards while taking into consideration the differences in the composition of households, the INSEE calculates in terms of 'units of consumption' (UC). A single person is equal to 1 UC, a couple 1.5 UC, a child of less than 14 years 0.3 UC, etc.

[125] Laurent Cordonnier, *Pas de pitié pour les gueux: Sur les théories économiques du chômage* (Paris: Raisons d'agir, 2000), p. 17.

particularly established that, between 1998 and 2005, 0.1% of the richest households had seen their income increase by 32%, whereas for 90% of households the global increase was only 4.6%. The investigation of the INSEE confirms this phenomenon by bringing it up to date.

Contrary to what some claim, fiscal pressure is, besides, not as strong on big fortunes that have the means to structure their capital and thus to conceal part of their incomes. 'Is it possible to ask a taxpayer to give to the state more than half of his income?' Nicolas Sarkozy had asked in the summer of 2007, with a feigned indignation, to justify his reform of the 'tax shield'[126] within the framework of the TEPA[127] law. The tax rates on the incomes of the richest is in fact very far from being confiscatory. According to the INSEE, it is on average 20%, and reaches 25% only for those who receive more than 82,000 euros a month in incomes. That is very far from the famous 'fiscal shield' of 50%, which concerns only a handful of taxpayers.[128] Besides, the essential part of the revenues of the very rich does not come from taxable salaries (that is to say, from their work), but from their investments and capital gains (that is to say, from the work of others), of which a good part is covered up thanks to the 'tax loopholes' and tax havens, which considerably diminishes the taxation that they could otherwise be subjected to.

The situation is the same in the United States, where the revenues of the richest 1% (those who earn more than 1.3 million dollars each year) have more than doubled between 1979 and 2006. This 1% of the population receives the equivalent of 21% of the gross national product (compared to 8% in 1980) and holds more than 35% of the national wealth (around

---

126 A tax shield is an allowable deduction from one's taxable income. Since interest payments on debts are tax deductible, taking on debt creates a tax shield, and thus can increase the value of a business.—Ed.

127 The acronym for Travail, Emploi et Pouvoir d'Achat, or Labour, Employment, and Purchasing Power.—Ed.

128 The reform of the 'tax shield' was also supposed to make those who had expatriated themselves for fiscal reasons to return to France. But the anticipated massive return did not take place: 246 in 2007, 312 in 2008. As for the number of fiscal exiles, it remains rather stable: 719 in 2007, 821 in 2008. According to a CSA [Conseil supérieur de l'audio-visuel] survey that appeared in April 2010 in *Le Parisien*, 67% of the French were hostile to the 'fiscal shield'.

17 trillion dollars). At the same time, 50% of the households (around 60 million families) hold only 2.5% of this same national wealth. The number of poor across the Atlantic has now reached 43.6 million people (5.7 million more than in 2009), or close to 15% of the total population. Officially there are 9.5% unemployed (17.1% if one adds to it the part-time employees and those who have left the working population), more than 50 million Americans receive no unemployment benefits, and 38 million of them manage to survive only thanks to food stamps.

Thus a 'global superclass' has been constituted in the world, whose number was estimated at being around 6,000 people by David Rothkopf — out of six billion inhabitants of the Earth.[129] This global 'hyperclass', whose core is evidently constituted by the financial elite, leads a transnational and segregated existence. It possesses its own places of residence and for vacation, as well as its networks of meetings and mutual aid. It frequents the same places of leisure. Its way of life, cosmopolitan and nomadic, is of an incestuous style: 'The individuals who participate in the new international elite have more interests in common with each other than they have with the middle classes or the poor with whom they share a nationality.'[130]

The widening of inequalities in fact brings about an aggravation of social segregation, whose effects are also seen in France. 'The richest and most educated families', emphasises the economist Éric Maurin, 'have never been so active in the educational and residential markets; they have never fled with so much diligence from the proximity of the working classes.' Michel Pinçon and Monique Pinçon-Charlot confirm this: 'Unlike the poor, the rich remain among themselves because they choose to. ... They mobilise to preserve the integrity of their roads, their quarters, their chic suburbs, their holiday spots. ... The families see to it, particularly in school, that their children associate withthe youth of other social milieus as little as possi-

---

129 David Rothkopf, *Superclass: The Global Power Elite and the World They Are Making* (New York: Farrar, Straus and Giroux, 2008).

130 Gérard Dussouy, *Les théories de la mondialité: Traité de relations internationales*, vol. 3 (Paris: L'Harmattan, 2009), p. 84. Cf. also Jeff Faux, *The Global Class War* (New York: John Wiley, 2006).

ble. The bourgeoisie thus declares itself as a class conscious of itself and its interests.'[131]

At the other extreme of the income scale we find the working classes, who may be 'modest' or 'poor'. Under this label of 'working classes' one generally understands the 'wage-earning worker', including labourers (23.2% of the working population) and office workers (28.6%). They combine lowness of social and professional status, narrowness of economic resources, and distance from cultural capital. Defined thus, these classes — one forgets too often — remain the majority in France, since they represent 51.8% of those who work.[132] Their resources are weak to the extent that, while the average salary rose by 12.3% from 1996 to 2006, the average salary (which separates the population into two equal halves) rose by only 3.5% in the same period, and reached 1,510 euros per month in 2007. As for the salaries of 50% of the lowest-paid French, their salaries have not increased at all since 1999.

In 2007, during his election campaign, Nicolas Sarkozy committed himself to reducing poverty by a third at the start of his five-year term. The opposite that has been realised. The number of people living below the poverty line (fixed at 60% of the average standard of living, or 950 euros per month) has today exceeded the level of 8 million people, or 13.4% of the population, for the first time. Of this number half has a standard of living lower than 720 euros per month. This explains why the number of meals served by the 'Restos du Coeur'[133] has grown from 8.5 million in 1986 to 10 million in 2009. One in five adults in France is now poor, and 45% of poor people are younger than 25. Let us add that more than 150,000 young

---

[131] Michel Pinçon and Monique Pinçon-Charlot, interview in *Télérama*, 20 September 2010.

[132] Cf. Éric Dupin, 'Des milieux populaires entre déception et défection', *Le Monde diplomatique*, April 2010, pp. 4–5.

[133] A French charity that distributes hot meals to the needy.—Ed.

people leave the school system without diplomas each year, and that a third of them will still not have any work five years later.[134]

A survey of TNS Sofres-Logica[135] that appeared in *Le Pèlerin* on 14 October 2010 reveals that almost one in five Frenchmen (18%) is today considered to be poor or very poor. Among the remaining 82%, the percentage of those who fear 'falling one day into poverty' rises to more than a third (37%). In total, it is thus almost half of the French who think they are already poor or are fearful of becoming so. This anguish before the future spares nobody: 41% of the merchants, artisans, and bosses of small businesses, 43% of couples with children, and 44% of 25–34-year-olds fear becoming poor. Nearly two-thirds (65%) of those surveyed think that the standard of living of the children of today will be lower than that of their own generation.

This study is also revealing concerning the anxiety of the middle classes. But the notion of 'middle classes' has always been quite vague. Sociologists tend to use profession and social category as its criterion, whereas economists are first of all interested in the distribution of incomes. Moreover, those who find themselves in the rich categories are often reluctant to be classified at the top of the scale of incomes, so much so that among the 20% of the richest people, 79% consider that they too are part of the middle classes. According to a study of the Centre d'analyse et de prévision,[136] between two-thirds and three-fourths of the French people consider themselves members of the middle class, the latter then being able to represent up to 80% of the general population. The Centre de recherche pour l'étude et l'observation des conditions de vie (CREDOC),[137] for its part, defines

---

134 It is a question here of an international phenomenon. In 2009, the unemployment of the young in the world reached its highest level ever recorded, with 81 million 15–24-year-olds without work, or an unemployment rate of 13%. In 2008, 152 million youth of the same age category earned less than one euro per day. In the United States, the unemployment of young people now reaches 18%.

135 Taylor Nelson-Sofres and Logica is are leading market research companies in France.—Ed.

136 The Centre d'analyse et de prévision (Centre for Analysis and Forecast) is a think-tank of the French Ministry of Foreign Affairs—Ed.

137 The Research Centre for the Study and Observation of Living Conditions.—Ed.

the middle classes as those earning between 1,120 and 2,600 euros every month, 30% of them having a monthly income of less than 1,750 euros for a single person. They constitute a population benefiting from a stable income, a relatively guaranteed social protection capable of ensuring a good education to its children, and able to allow itself certain leisure activities. Thus defined, this category represented 52.1% of the population in 2000, as compared to 47.9% in 1981.

The purchasing power of the middle classes has been rapidly increasing for a long time: it rose by 83% between 1970 and 2004. One therefore cannot speak of 'impoverishment'. But their standard of living only progresses increasingly slowly (between 1998 and 2006, the median monthly income increased for them by only 24 euros a year, whereas it increased by 27% for the highest incomes) and they now live under an increased pressure since, since the 1980s, their basic expenses have been increasing more quickly than their incomes. Among the middle classes, one in two people lives on 1,467 euros a month after paying all their taxes, a sum lower than the median salary. Of this sum, 38% (compared to 21% in 1979) is devoted to basic expenses: rent, service charges, electricity, telephone, insurance, and so on, the other unavoidable expenses (food, transport, education, health) representing, on average, 615 euros. Once these deductions are made, only 294 euros per month is left for leisure activities, clothes, furnishings, appliances, and savings. The result: in 2008, among the middle classes having a 'median budget', 48% did not go on vacation, 34% did not have a car, and 37% avoided going to the cinema. At that time, the CREDOC specifies that 72% of the lower middle classes declared that 'they had to regularly impose restrictions on themselves concerning certain items in their budget', compared to 64% in 1980.

In total, the basic expenses of the middle classes have almost doubled in 30 years: 21% of the budget of the lower middle classes compared to 38% today. In comparison, between 1979 and 2005, the weight of basic expenses moved from 19% to 29% for the rich categories, and from 24%

to 48% for the poor categories. Once the unavoidable expenses have been paid, only 80 euros remains for 10% of the poorest to live on.

For the last ten years, the fiscal policy in France has consisted in large part of reducing taxes for the wealthiest and in having increasing recourse to indirect taxes. Besides, for a long time it has been the VAT that has been essential for the fiscal receipts: 131.7 billion euros in 2008 (50.6% of the fiscal receipts of the state) compared to 51.2 and 15.6 billion euros for the income tax and the company tax (16.8% and 4.5% of the fiscal receipts of the state). Today, only half the French people (54% in 2007) pay income taxes. Indirect taxes, like the VAT on consumption or the tax on petrol, increase the relative inequalities of income, for, if the richest consume more and globally pay more indirect taxes than everyone else, the level of these taxes, when viewed as a fraction of their income, is clearly lower than what the poorest pay. Since VAT strikes all consumers indiscriminately, the budget of the state is based above all on the middle and working classes.

The working classes had been the big losers of the last three decades. It is now the turn of the middle classes. They are in fact more affected because they do not benefit from the subsidies and social aids allocated to the lowest working classes. A conference organised in the Senate in 2007 has established that the most 'unfavoured' category of the population today is those whose incomes are situated between 40% and 100% of the average income, that is to say, the lower stratum of the middle class, the extreme petite bourgeoisie — the poorest benefiting from an increase in income of around 20%, thanks to social transfers.

Another recent study of the CREDOC[138] confirms the 'disenchantment' of the middle classes, which have been the first to suffer the consequences of the crisis and experience the widening of inequalities even more painfully. 'Without denying the importance of the difficulties of the working classes and of those who have to deal with marginalisation', writes Louis

---

138 *Consommation et modes de vie*, 219, March 2009.

Chauvel, 'it is the turn of the central categories of society to experience a form of civilisational precariousness.'[139]

By general agreement, the 'social elevator' has now broken down. While in the past one did not leave the middle class once one had entered it, that is no longer true today. This is the direct result of the increase in professional precariousness and the degradation of the labour market: the multiplication of part-time positions and of jobs of limited duration save the high incomes but weaken the middle classes. In the 1960s, 12 years were necessary for the middle classes to reach the standard of living of the rich classes. Today 35 years are necessary. This is the reason why the middle classes have the impression of falling behind in comparison to the richest.

Often perceived as a 're-proletarisation', the lowering of status is indeed real. Camille Peugny thus observes a phenomenon of 'downward mobility' which today affects 25% of the segment of society aged 35–39 years, compared to 18% twenty years ago. 'Many young people live less well than their parents', he writes, evoking a 'sacrificed generation' which has 'never been so qualified and which has never been worse integrated into the world of labour'.[140] For a young person, this lowering of status can take the form of an unhinging with regard to the social situation of his parents, as well as of a gap with regard to that which his own level of education could allow him to hope for. The young are in fact confronted with a considerable rate of unemployment despite their diplomas. Nowadays, to accept a job which has no connection to one's level of education is to run the high risk of remaining there all one's life. Many also accept to work increasingly more for fear of falling into unemployment once again.

The middle class, which has already crumbled considerably, feels this sentiment of a lowering of status powerfully, and this has been confirmed

---

[139] 'Classes moyennes, le grand retournement', *Le Monde*, 3 May 2006, p. 24.
[140] Camille Peugny, *Le déclassement* (Paris: Grasset, 2009).

by all observers for the last fifteen years.[141] It knows that it has nothing more to expect either from Europe or from globalisation in terms of employment or purchasing power. It has understood that the 'European construction' is no longer anything but the means of imposing neoliberal reforms on the peoples whose objective is to adapt the European societies to the demands of globalisation. All the studies reveal a profound general malaise among it that is being aggravated by the loss of its bearings and fear of the future. These very bitter, depressed people have the impression of being perpetually duped, without however being truly in revolt. Let us remember that the French consumption of tranquilising drugs multiplied twofold between 1992 and 2007.

This erosion of the middle classes is confirmed today almost everywhere, in Europe as in the United States, but also in Argentina, Brazil, Chile, South Korea, the Ivory Coast, and so on. In the United States, where the 'dumpies' ('downwardly mobile professionals', according to the definition given by *Business Week*) tend to replace the 'yuppies', one witnesses a large-scale regression of 'white-collar workers' towards the bottom. In this country, the median income has increased by 20% over the last twenty years, but property costs have risen by 56% and that of education from 43% to 60%. As for health expenses, they have risen by 155%!

In short, everywhere the inequalities widen between the countries as well as within each country. The rich are increasingly richer, the poor increasingly poorer, and the middle classes are threatened with a drop in status. The question that arises is to know how one came to this. The answer has to do with the recent history of capitalism.

In the capitalist system of the nineteenth century, the class struggle was a zero-sum game: everything gained by one class was automatically lost by the other — whence the ferocity of the system. In the following century,

---

141 Cf. Robert Castel, *From Manual Workers to Wage Laborers: Transformation of the Social Question* (New Brunswick, New Jersey: Transaction Publishers, 2003); *L'insecurité sociale* (Paris: Seuil, 2003); Louis Chauvel, *Les classes moyennes à la dérive* (Paris: Seuil, 2006); Robert Rochefort, 'Classes moyennes, la dégringolade', *Le Point*, 26 June 2008, p. 75.

principally after the 1930s, the advent of Fordism introduced a major revolution, causing the entire system to move into a second phase. Fordism was based on the fact that production does not have any purpose if it is not consumed, which means that it is necessary to pay the workers suitably if one wishes them to buy the merchandise that one seeks to sell to them. In the Fordist system, the fraction of added value which the capitalists give up to pay it in the form of salaries, returns to them during the purchase of goods and services by the wage-earners, the wage-earners thus simultaneously representing a cost and a profit. From that time, a consensus could arise. In exchange for security and an almost constantly rising salary, the workers abandoned their most revolutionary demands. The syndicalists became at the same time reformist. The Fordist system was, besides, reconciled with the welfare state, even if the latter curbed the financial sphere by striving to include the economic dynamic within a framework that was still national insofar as it allowed at least the consolidation of social rights and the continued growth of salaries. A relative balance could thus be established between the interests of the markets, productivity, competition, and a certain number of social protections — capitalism no longer impoverishing men but multiplying the number of the poor (to multiply the number of the poor it is necessary that a company be richer). It is this system that dominated social relations until the 1970s.

It was also in this period, which began in the period between the wars, that the middle class progressively expanded, principally at the expense of the working classes. Its essential characteristic was that once one entered into the middle class, one never came down from it. During the Fordist period, the middle classes in fact prospered, for, thanks to their growing purchasing power, they contributed to the good functioning of a system characterised by mass production and mass consumption. They played an important role in the creation and sustenance of demand by absorbing increasingly more vital quantities of standardised goods and services, but also by accepting to pay for quality products at a higher price, which favoured innovation and investment. Further, the means of their parents improved slowly and their children were thus able to undertake longer studies at a higher level, which placed a highly qualified workforce whom the businesses required on the labour market. Besides which the alliance between the middle classes and industrial capitalism was so much stronger, in that the areas of production and consumption largely coincided: that which was produced in the North was for the most part consumed in the North. In other words, the middle classes became denser at the same time that the capitalist system was fully promoted. The revolutionary parties had disappeared, and the syndicates no longer expressed anything but marginal demands, leaving the political class to find itself relatively in accord with the electorate.

But the middle classes, who ally with capital when they prosper, are on the way to losing their status when their interests begin to diverge from those of capital. The cyclical character of the dynamic of the middle classes seems to have to be explained by the fact that, after having been a developmental factor that contributed to the rapid growth of capital, they become, at the end of a certain time, a brake on the growth of profits. The public powers then tend to organise their decline.[142]

Fordism began to disappear in the course of the 1970s. The end of the monetary system established by Bretton Woods, which ordained the end of the system of fixed exchange rates in 1971, the petrol shocks of 1973 and 1979, stagflation, the crisis of the countries of the South in 1982, the collapse of the Soviet system, and finally economic and financial globalisation, have ended in a veritable disconnection of the interests of the middle classes from those of capital. There was a change of epoch when the interventions of the state, which had played a very important role in the formations of the national markets in the period when capitalism still had a national anchoring, were revealed to be incompatible with the internationalisation of the markets that was realised within the framework of globalisation. A new, entirely deterritorialised capitalism was set up whose driving forces were the

---

142 Cf. Bernard Conte, 'Néolibéralisme et euthanasie des classes moyennes', online text, October 2010.

big international firms and the financial markets, but which also benefited from the new American hegemony. There resulted from this a considerable development of international commerce, whose rates of growth quickly exceeded that of national wealth. One then witnessed the end of the social-democratic consensus which had marked the immediate post-war years, a consensus which had become so much more unnecessary in that, the Soviet Union having disappeared at almost the same time, the 'Communist danger' was no longer relevant. It is from this time that the market found itself in a position to claim to regulate the economy of the global society thanks to the rapid liberalisation of international cash flows.

Henceforth, as Bernard Conte explains very well, since growth is no longer self-centred, surpluses are no longer automatically redistributed: 'Free-trade permits the inundation of the markets with products at low cost which undercut national production, revealing their deficient "competitiveness". To become competitive (again) implies the lowering of direct and indirect production costs. This process includes the reduction of real salaries, social benefits and, more generally, "clientelist" expenses (related to corruption) and expenses related to the welfare state. Under the pretext of competition, it is a question of raising profits again. In order to do that, it is convenient to adjust the national economic and social structures to the rules of "*laisser-faire, laisser-passer*"[143] extended to the whole planet. Among the population, as the poor are too poor and the rich are exempted, it is on the middle class that the major burden of adjustment will rest. Thus, the middle class becomes the "enemy" of financial capitalism, for its unjustified existence — since elsewhere populations carry out the same productive tasks at less cost — reduces profits. Capitalism denounces the compromise concluded previously and has the euthanasia of the parasitical middle class carried out.'[144]

---

[143] This phrase was adopted by the French economist Vincent de Gournay (1712–1759). Literally meaning 'Let do, let pass', Gournay used it to describe an economic system that is free of government interference.—Ed.

[144] *Ibid.*

To do this the intervention of the state, henceforth subject to the principles of 'world governance', has shown itself to be indispensable. It has readopted the form of a systematic regulation, a destruction of social gains, an erosion of public powers, a reform of pensions or taxes of which the middle classes have been the first victims, on the basis of a powerful comeback of the neoliberal ideology which had already inspired the reforms of Thatcher and Reagan. By the same stroke, a gap was dug between the middle classes and the ruling class, the latter not ceasing to set up policies contrary to the interests of its traditional electorate, which resulted, on the one hand, in the rise of abstention and, on the other, in a crisis of the global legitimacy of the New Class.

Endowed with a new ferocity, this capitalism of the third type, sometimes called 'turbo-capitalism' or 'neoliberal capitalism', sanctions the primal role that the financial markets today play in the functioning of the economy. It is thus essentially a financial capitalism: since the beginning of the 1980s, financial transactions count for more than the invested capitals in the production of goods, the purchase and sale of fictional capital on the stock markets themselves counting for more than the productive development of real capital. Before the crisis of 2008, for example, of 3,200 billion dollars that were exchanged daily in the world, less than 3% corresponded to real goods or services, which gives us a measure of the disconnection between the speculative economy and the real economy. The liberal justification for this phenomenon is that the financial markets constitute the only mechanism for the efficient allocation of capital, for which reason one should not hinder or even seek to regulate their functioning. This theoretical postulate (called informational efficiency) is baseless: the financial crisis of 2008 has indeed shown that the markets are not efficient and that financial competition does not necessarily produce fair prices, but, on the contrary, very often inadequate prices. The major error of this theory is to transfer to financial markets the theory of markets of ordinary goods, based on the classical law of supply and demand. Regarding the financial markets, when the price of a security rises it is common to observe not a lowering but a rise in demand, for the simple reason that the rise of the price signifies an increased return for those possessing the security in question, due to the fact of the capital gain that they can thus realise. This is the very source of the 'speculative bubbles': a cumulative rise in prices which sustains itself until the unforeseeable but inevitable incident that provokes the reversal of expectations and the crash.

From the Maastricht Treaty (1992), we have besides witnessed the establishment of the euro, which was introduced into the inter-bank exchanges in 1999 and, in 2002, in the form of coins and notes. This creation of a new form of money, which was in itself a good thing, made no sense except on the double condition of it being accompanied by a customs union and of taking into consideration the disparity in the economic levels between the European countries, which has not been the case. The single European currency has imposed a single interest rate on sixteen economies whose needs were different, whereas, in the absence of an objective aimed at achieving an optimal exchange rate that is impossible to determine, it became the monetary variable of international adjustment of the American deficits. As for the abolition of the customs protections, it had the effect of placing the entirety of the French and European wage-earners in competition with more than 3 billion inhabitants (1.3 billion Chinese, 1 billion Indians, 580 million inhabitants of other countries) whose salaries are immeasurably lower than theirs. This resulted in commercial relations that led to dumping conditions, a series of delocalisations and, in France, a veritable industrial haemorrhaging, since we are now losing between 800 and 1,000 industrial jobs per working day! (In 2006, there were no more than 3.9 million industrial jobs, compared to 5.9 million in 1970.) Today, being clearly overvalued in relation to the dollar, the euro is in the process of choking a part of European industry by flattening its export margins.

The policy of a general dismantling of regulations on the exchanges of goods and capitals has been the essential vector of globalisation. In a post-Fordist system, the organisation of production becomes a network of interconnected cashflows in an increasingly more competitive economy. The process of transnationalisation ends in the establishment of a systemic coherence where the capitals, goods, and technologies have been rendered mobile as never before by the activity of the large companies and the markets. 'The mobility of capital, so crucial for this transnational system, is effected in the form of direct foreign investments and participations in the growth of private or public debt, which finally cause a rupture of the national credit accumulation system.'[145]

Maurice Allais had rightly seen the harmful role played by 'multinationals which are, along with the stock exchange and banking milieus, the principal beneficiaries of an economic mechanism which has enriched them while it has impoverished the majority of the French, but also the world's, population' ('Letter to the French', in *Marianne*). This Nobel Prizewinner for economics estimated that globalisation and international free-tradeism have destroyed a third of the income once earned by the French. Taking into consideration the multiplying effects of industrial employment on global employment, delocalisations and the pressure of free trade seem besides to have brought about a 3.5% reduction in the working population.

The downward pressure on salaries, already brought about by the resort to immigration in the workforce, has resulted in the conjunction of two essential factors. The first was evidently the institution of international free-tradeism, which principally affected Europe and instantly resulted in an entire series of delocalisations. 'The financial leaders have the highest incomes on an international level, even while delocalising the industrial, and then the tertiary, jobs to zones where work is least paid. The Chinese or Filipino workers set the standard and the French workers who are laid off are faced with replacement jobs hundreds or thousands of kilometres

---

[145] Jérôme Maucourant and Bruno Tinel, 'Avènement du néocapitalisme — d'une internationalisation à une transnationalisation des économies?', online text, 2010.

away from home, at a local fee that is a pittance.'[146] In this way the economies have found themselves involved in a spiral of rampant inflation in salaries, thus of a contraction of purchasing power that was masked for a while thanks to the widespread granting of credit which, even while creating a 'false middle class', has aggravated the indebtedness of individuals.

The other factor is the shareholder constraint. This results from the fact that, in the present system, it is fundamentally the businesses which finance the shareholders, whereas before it was the opposite. The rise in power of shareholder value henceforth nourishes the idea that business is above all at the service of the shareholders — beginning with powerful shareholders such as investment funds — whose desire it should respect for a return on investment that is as fast and high as possible (a rate of return on one's capital of the order of 15% to 25% is henceforth the norm). This holds even when that results in a need for the lowering of salaries, delocalisations, and layoffs, but also in a slowing down of business investments — the simultaneous curbing of investment and consumption ending in an endemic unemployment. 'The person with a "business" morale has thus been instrumentalised and lowered to the rank of a profit-making machine.'[147]

The two phenomena have resulted in the rise of a mass structural (and no longer temporary) unemployment since the 1980s, to which productivity gains have also contributed. At the same time, the share of incomes from work in the GDP has not stopped diminishing, to the advantage of incomes from capital. The essential trait of this vast process of 'Third Worldisation' of developed economies[148] has been the lowering of the share of salaries in the added value, that is to say, the rise in the rates of exploitation, in a context where capital can henceforth set the forces of labour in competition with one another at the international level.[149] The global

---

146 Michel Pinçon-Charlot and Monique Pinçon-Charlot, *Le président des riches: Enquête sur l'oligarchie dans la France de Nicolas Sarkozy* (Paris: Zones, 2010).

147 Jean-Luc Gréau, interview with *Le Choc du mois*, May 2010, p. 36.

148 Cf. Bernard Conte, *La tiers-mondialisation de la planète* (Bordeaux: Presses universitaires de Bordeaux, 2009).

149 Cf. Michel Husson, *Un pur capitalisme* (Lausanne: Page deux, 2010).

society, henceforth, no longer resembles a pyramid, as during the time of the Thirty Glorious Years — when the profits accumulated at the summit of the pyramid ended by partly flowing downwards once again towards the base, in conformity with the 'theory of development' formulated by Alfred Sauvy[150] — but an hourglass, with the rich always richer at the summit, the poor always poor at the base, and, in the middle, the increasingly choked middle classes. It will be noted that this widening of inequalities itself belies the thesis that is at the heart of free-tradeism and the ideology of *laisser-faire*, according to which, in a context of free competition, people receive revenue that is proportional to their contribution to the process of production. In reality, the more free trade extends, the more the inequalities between incomes grow.

But the divergence of incomes is also the result of the system of remuneration at the heart of business, which is itself linked to the evolution of the structure of employment which, in the course of the last decades, has been considerable.

At the beginning of the 1960s the labour force in France was very predominantly masculine (in the 1962 census, one counted in the metropolis 19 million people with jobs, two-thirds of whom were men), rather blue-collar and not very qualified. In the majority of families only the head of the household performed a job outside the home. That was during the reign of the large-scale industrial enterprise marked by a method of work organisation of the Fordist or Taylorist[151] type, with, essentially, work contracts of indefinite duration and full-time hours. Today, employment has completely 'exploded', whether it is a question of job statutes and situations, rates of unemployment, work durations and rhythms, modes of remuneration, or productive units. Employment has become urbanised and tertiarised,

---

150 Alfred Sauvy (1898–1990) was a French anthropologist best-known for having coined the term 'Third World'.—Ed.

151 Fordism is the notion of mass production as pioneered by the assembly lines of Henry Ford, who believed that his workers should be paid sufficiently to purchase the automobiles they themselves were building. Taylorism, or scientific management, was developed by Frederick Taylor in an effort to increase economic efficiency by subjecting labour to a larger and more centralised methods of managerial systems.—Ed.

but also feminised, given the massive entry of women into the working world, which has allowed capital to lower average salaries (the norm for a household henceforth consisting of two salaries instead of one). The restrictions associated with work have also changed in nature with the rise of precariousness and flexibility (less work time but more commuting time, less physical fatigue but more stress and suicides).[152]

The number of people having a job today approaches 26 million and is distributed almost equally between men and women. Jobs nevertheless remain largely 'sexist': more than four out of five blue-collar workers are men, whereas almost four out of five office workers are women; there are only 15% women in the industrial sector, notably the automobile industry and construction (9%), whereas there are 75% in education and health. There are hardly more than 6 million blue-collar workers (less than one out of four jobs) whereas there were still 7.4 million in 1962, which at that time constituted 39% of the working population. As for the peasants, they do not represent more than 1% of the working population. The salaried non-blue-collar professions have increased steadily, on the other hand, with the development of the tertiary sector and the service industry, as well as the rise of communication technologies, the share of office workers growing by 10% (18.3% in 1962, 28.4% in 2007) and that of white-collar workers by more than 11% (from 4.7% to 15.8%). The near-disappearance of rural France has gone hand-in-hand with the predominance of the tertiary, which now constitutes three-quarters of all jobs, whether it is a question of competitive tertiary (business) or of public tertiary (non-business). This is also what explains the rapid rise in the wage rates: 56% at the beginning of the twentieth century, 72% in 1962, almost 90% today. The share of young people in employment has, on the other hand, sharply diminished, especially on account of the prolongation of education: the under-30s today represent less than a fifth of the working population, compared to more

---

152 For countries like Switzerland or Sweden, where systematic surveys have been conducted in this field (which was never the case in France), the cost of stress and illnesses produced by the rhythms of work is equal to 3% of the GDP.

than a quarter at the beginning of the 1960s. At the other extreme of life, the share in employment of wage-earners over 50 years old has likewise not stopped diminishing, working life now being concentrated in the intermediary ages.[153]

Finally, an essential difference in relation to the 1960s is the strong rise in unemployment: less than 2% in 1962, almost 10% today. It has gone hand-in-hand with job precariousness, the rise in importance of temporary jobs (fixed-term contracts, temporary employment, etc.), which today represent 15% of the salaried employment, and the increase in part-time work, which was almost nonexistent in the 1960s but now represents 18% of it. This makes one think that the irregular forms of employment are tending to become 'normal'. The degradation of professional statuses is in fact becoming the rule. The less qualified blue-collar workers and the young who try to enter the labour market for the first time are the most affected by this new salarial condition, 'precariousness' (Robert Castel), which is paradoxically tending to become the permanent status for many workers. 'The working class milieus and the lower section of the middle classes hardly possess the means to deal with the destabilisation of social relations', remarks the sociologist Alain Mergier.[154]

Conclusion: the search for profits today demands an over-exploitation of the employable person to extract a capital gain that is endlessly expanding. When the cost of work becomes too high, the rise in productivity allows the dismissal of surplus workers, leading to unemployment or misery. Globalisation weakens the power of trade unions, whose action continues to fall within an essentially national framework. It allows employers to systematically resort to blackmail, by forcing the workers to accept stagnations or reductions in their salaries on pain of seeing their jobs eliminated alto-

---

153 The weight of those over 50 nevertheless tends to rise today, but more for demographic reasons (they are henceforth the most numerous) than by virtue of a rise in their rates of work. The deferment of the retirement age to 62 years should amplify this tendency.

154 Cf. Philippe Guibert and Alain Mergier, *Le descenseur social: Enquête sur les milieux populaires* (Paris: Plon, 2006). Cf. also Christophe Guilluy and Christophe Noyé, *Atlas des nouvelles fractures sociales en France* (Paris: Autrement, 2006).

gether and their businesses delocalised, which further aggravates the reduction of consumption and domestic demand. The capitalism of the present is returning to its initial savage state, but in a perspective henceforth deterritorialised, globalisation having allowed it to throw overboard all the 'controls' capable of regulating it; quite simply, all the social gains that a century of struggles by the working class had imposed on it.

One finds oneself here before an international dynamic, but which has taken particular forms in France, most especially since the accession to power of Nicolas Sarkozy. One knows in particular how the present head of state has worked, since his election, at 'decomplexifying' political power in relation to the financial powers, he himself providing an example of a happy fascination for money. 'One of the dimensions of this ambition', writes Roland Hureaux, 'is to kill what remains to us of shame regarding money: our old "Catholic foundation." ... An old aristocratic foundation also, which rendered rich people who were too indiscreet "parvenus." ... It is being suggested by the "bling-bling" ideology that this old foundation, which still characterises the French mentality, should be killed, for it is judged old-fashioned and archaic in a world dominated by the English language and the Anglo-Saxon and Protestant values.'[155]

From the indecent night at Le Fouquet's,[156] where all the members of the ruling class had come together to celebrate his election to the presidency of the Republic, from the bosses of the CAC 40[157] to the showbiz stars, to the reinforcement of the 'fiscal shield', from the vacations on yachts or private jet to the exemption of the inheritance tax, Nicolas Sarkozy has clearly positioned himself as the president of the rich, even if he could not have been elected without capturing the votes of the lower and average middle class, among whom he was able to exercise the lure of profit ('work more

---

155 Roland Hureaux, online text, *Liberté politique* site, 2 July 2010.

156 Le Fouquet's is a famed, historic restaurant located on the Champs-Élysées in Paris. It became associated with Nicolas Sarkozy after he celebrated his electoral victory there in 2007, and Sarkozy and his entourage continued to be associated with the restaurant in the French press thereafter.—Ed.

157 The Cotation Assistée en Continu 40 is a French stock market index.—Ed.

to gain more!'). 'The investiture of Nicolas Sarkozy', write Michel Pinçon and Monique Pinçon-Charlot, 'is that of social cynicism: money no longer needs to hide itself, it is the natural consecration of talent, courage, social utility, and all success. It is perfectly legitimate that the rich are rich, ever richer, and joined by the *nouveaux riches*, since all this accumulation is the very motor of the economy and of growth.'[158]

In their books, *Les ghettos du gotha* (*The Ghettoes of the Elite*) and *Le président des riches* (*The President of the Rich*), Michel Pinçon and Monique Pinçon-Charlot have well described the manner in which the connivance between political power and the world of business functions in an age when, everywhere in the world, liberal democracy is nothing more than an elected oligarchy that increasingly ignores the borders between the public and the private. In France, as in Italy, one notes the existence of an assumed, even declared, link between the executive power and money. The 'super-ego'[159] of public service is no longer active. 'In the past', notes Pierre Rosanvallon, 'the Republic was evidently not sheltered by connivances with the big economic interest, but the sentiment predominated that it was above that and that politico-financial affairs constituted serious problems. Today, there is an almost ingenuous loss of the sense of what the common good, the state, and the administration of the general interest, mean.'[160]

Taking into consideration the extent of public debts, all the European governments have today committed themselves to austerity policies, based on plans to drastically reduce public expenses, which are only a machine to produce unemployment and misery. Every time, in fact, it is the working classes and the middle classes who are called on to bear their cost. The number of public servants is already diminishing everywhere, threatening public services. Social allowances have been amputated, and the amount of pensions has been revised downwards. The number of non-reimbursed

---

158 *Le président des riches*.

159 In Freud's conception of psychology, the super-ego is that part of consciousness which contains those cultural norms and values which were passed down by one's parents.—Ed.

160 Pierre Rosanvallon, 'Le pouvoir contre l'intérêt général', interview in *Le Monde*, 21 September 2010, p. 19.

medications continues to grow. Unprecedented cuts have been effected in the defence budgets. Unemployment and job insecurity increase steadily. In France, from now until 2013, the government proposes to eliminate 40,000 positions in national education, 20,000 medical staff positions in the public hospitals, 10,000 positions in the police, and 20,000 positions in the army, whereas the expenses related to social welfare programmes will be reduced by 10%. With incredible cynicism, Sarkozy has even decreed the taxation of compensations paid for occupational accidents, which have, since December 2009, been considered as a taxable income! A form of dictatorship of the markets is thus being imposed everywhere.

All these choices are presented as being the product of developments against which one can do nothing, that is to say, as inevitable misfortunes. In reality, they are inevitable only in the ruling system — a system, for example, where the states should borrow at more than 3% from the banks, when these same banks are refinanced at rates fluctuating between 0.5% and 1%, by the European Central Bank (ECB) or the American Federal Reserve. This means, in the final analysis, that it is the markets which hold the key to the financing of states! Besides which these measures are doomed to failure since the countries that incur a major current deficit should, in order to respect their commitments in matters of debt, eventually come up with surpluses which they are today incapable of obtaining except by provoking a contraction of domestic demand equivalent to a deep and lasting recession. This is true most especially when their export capacities are reduced by the fact of the weakening of their competitiveness.

At the same time, of course, one forgets that the recent explosion in public debt is above all the consequence of the finance rescue plans and the recession provoked by the financial crisis of 2008.[161] 'The growth of public debt in Europe and the United States', a recent text recalled, 'is not the result of expansionist Keynesian policies or of extravagant social policies,

---

[161] The average public debt in the Eurozone was only 0.6% of the GDP in 2007, whereas it reached 7% in 2010. The public debt, in the same period, went from 66% to 84.5% of the GDP. As for the public deficit, it has multiplied threefold between September 2008 and December 2009, going from 52 billion to 145 billion euros.

but much rather of a policy in favour of a privileged strata: the "fiscal expenses" (lowering of taxes and contributions) increase the available income of those who have least need of it, who at the same time can increase their investments still more, especially in Treasury bonds, which are remunerated by interest from the tax deducted from all taxpayers. In sum, there is a mechanism of backward redistribution from the working classes to the wealthy classes being established via the public debt — whose counterpart is always private income.'[162] It is thus clearly the middle and working classes which are going to absorb the damages caused by the banks and the financial markets through the application of the old principle: 'privatisation of profits and socialisation of losses'.

Historically, the middle classes have often been at the source of revolutions. Threatened by loss of status, they have also in general been tempted by authoritarian solutions. That is the reason why, in the twentieth century, they gave broad support to fascisms. Today, they are obviously seduced by a mixture of liberal neopopulism and xenophobia. The majority of populist movements are, besides, nourished by this fear of loss of status by the petite bourgeoisie and of the lower strata of the middle class, which is added to the rancour of the working classes.

Whereas the Right defends the power of money without a second thought, the largest part of the Left has distanced itself from the people by joining the 'illegal immigration cause' while it is itself being directed by elites connected to globalisation, cut off from the low wage-earners of the private sector.[163] 'It is in a new alliance of the working classes and the middle classes', Jacques Sapir thinks, however, 'that the weapons of the defeat of

---

[162] Philippe Askenazy, Thomas Coutrot, André Orléan, and Henri Sterdyniak, 'Manifeste des économies atterrés', online text, 2010.

[163] Gaël Brustier and Jean-Philippe Huelin, authors of *Recherche le peuple désespérément* (Paris: Bourin, 2009), do not hesitate to speak of the 'proletariophobia' of one section of the French elites.

those that Alain Minc[164] represents, the richest and the most overfed, will be forged.'[165]

'The feeble turnout in the elections reveals a disarray so much more profound in that it decreases according to the social level', again write Michel Pinçon and Monique Pinçon-Charlot, who add: 'In the indistinct magma of contemporary thought, the struggle of classes is relegated to the dustbins of history. The notion of social class disappears from the politically correct language. Social movements are denounced as archaic. The rights wrested through great struggle by the workers in the battles of the past are becoming intolerable privileges for the jugglers of finance who, on a signal from the stock exchange, can rake in millions at the expense of the real economy.'

Towards a new class struggle? Yes, but only the rich conduct it now. That is why they have won so far.

---

[164] Alain Minc (b. 1949) is a French businessman who was an advisor to Nicolas Sarkozy. He has authored many books and is a member of a number of think tanks.—Ed.

[165] Jacques Sapir, 'Sortie de crise: une autre voie est possible', online text, *Contre-Info* site, 24 March 2010.

Immigration, the Reserve Army of Capital

In 1973, shortly before his death, President Pompidou recognised that he had opened the floodgates of immigration at the demand of a certain number of big bosses, such as Francis Bouygues,[166] who were desirous of benefiting from a docile workforce, cheap, deprived of class consciousness and all tradition of social struggles, in order to exercise a downward pressure on the salaries of French workers, to reduce their zeal for protest and, in addition, to break the unity of the labour movement. These big bosses, he emphasised, 'always want more'.

Forty years later, nothing has changed. At a time when no party of the government would risk demanding the further acceleration of the pace of immigration, only the bosses speak out for this, quite simply because it is still in their interest. The only difference is that the economic sectors concerned are now more numerous, going beyond the industrial or restaurant sectors to extend to professions that were once spared, such as engineers or information technology specialists.

France, one knows, has heavily relied on immigration since the nineteenth century. The immigrant population already represented 800,000 people in 1876, 1.2 million persons in 1911. At first the magnet of Italian and Belgian immigrations, the French industry later attracted the Polish,

---

[166] Francis Bouygues (1922–1993) was a French businessman and film producer who founded the industrial group Bouygues SA in 1952, which is a blue chip company in the CAC 40.

then the Spanish and the Portuguese. 'This immigration, not very qualified and not unionised, is going to allow the employer to exempt himself from the growing restrictions of the labour law.'[167] In 1924, a General Society for Immigration (SGI) was even created at the initiative of the Committee of Coal Mines and the large-scale farmers of the northeast. It opened employment offices in Europe which functioned as a suction pump. In 1931, one could count 2.7 million foreigners in France, or 6.6% of the total population. France showed the highest rates of immigration in the world at that time (515 for 10,000 inhabitants). 'A good means for an entire section of the employers to place a downward pressure on salaries. ... From this time, capitalism seeks to place the workforce in competition by calling on salarial reserve armies.'[168]

In the aftermath of the Second World War, immigrants would come with increasing frequency from the countries of the Maghreb; Algeria first of all, then Morocco. Lorries chartered by big businesses would come in their hundreds to recruit locally. From 1962 to 1974, close to two million additional immigrations would thus enter France, of which 550,000 were recruited by the National Office of Immigration (ONI), an organisation run by the state, but secretly controlled by the employers. Since then, the wave has not stopped growing.

'When there is a shortage of workforce in a sector', François-Laurent Balssa explains, 'one of two things happens: either one increases the salaries, or one calls upon a foreign workforce. It is generally the second option which will continue to be chosen by the National Council of French Employers (CNPF),[169] then, from 1988, by the Movement for French Enterprises (Medef)[170] which succeeded it. This was a choice demonstrating a desire for short-term profits, which had to proportionately slow down

---

167 François-Laurent Balssa, 'Un choix salarial pour les grandes entreprises', *Le Spectacle du monde*, October 2010, p. 42.

168 *Ibid.*, p. 43.

169 Conseil national du patronat français.—Ed.

170 Mouvement des entreprises de France.—Ed.

the improvement of the instruments of production and innovation in industrial matters. At the same time, in fact, the example of Japan shows that the rejection of immigration in favour of autochthonous employment permitted that country to accomplish its technological revolution before the majority of its Western competitors.'[171]

Immigration was thus from the beginning an employer phenomenon. It continues to be that today. Those who want ever more immigration are the big businesses. This immigration is in accordance with the spirit of capitalism itself, which tends towards the abolition of borders ('*laissez faire, laissez passer*'). 'Obeying the logic of social dumping', François-Laurent Balssa continues, 'a market of "low cost" work has thus been created with poorly qualified illegal immigrants acting as a stop-gap. As if the big employers and the extreme Left had shaken hands, the former to dismantle the welfare state which is too expensive in their eyes, the latter to destroy the nation-state, too archaic.'[172] That is the reason why the Communist Party and the CGT[173] — which have radically changed orientation since — fought against the liberal principle of opening borders until 1981, in the name of the defence of the interests of the working class.

'Let men, but also capitals and goods, pass; such is the doctrine of the European Commission. Better: let men pass in order to make the movement of capitals and merchandise more profitable', writes Éric Zemmour, who recalls that 'the very important migratory movements of the last twenty years have been one of the major constituents of an economic growth without inflation, since this continual flow of workers at low cost has hung like a lead weight on the salaries of Western workers.'[174] Michèle Tribalat observes for her part that 'immigration modifies the division of the economic pie, and this undeniable observation has much to do with the fact

---

171 *Ibid.*, p. 44.
172 *Ibid.*, p. 45.
173 Confédération Générale du Travail, the French Trade Union Federation.—Ed.
174 *Le Spectacle du monde*, September 2010, pp. 16–17.

that some are in favour of high immigration, whereas others seek to restrict or stop it.'[175]

For once well-inspired, the liberal Philippe Nemo confirms these observations: 'There are economic leaders in Europe who dream of making a cheap, capable workforce come, first to occupy certain jobs for which the local workforce is insufficient, then to considerably pressure the salaries of the other European workers downwards. These lobbies, who have all the means to make themselves heard, both by the national governments and by the Commission in Brussels, are thus in favour both of immigration in general and in an enlargement of Europe which would considerably facilitate the migrations of work. They are right from their own point of view, that is to say, according to a purely economic rationale. ... The problem is that one cannot reason here according to a purely economic rationale since the influx into Europe of exogenous populations also has heavy sociological consequences. If the capitalists in question pay little attention to this problem, it is perhaps that they generally enjoy economic benefits from immigration without themselves suffering the social damages. Thanks to the money earned by their businesses, whose profitability is in this way assured, they can live in beautiful quarters, leaving their less fortunate compatriots to manage with the non-native populations in the disinherited suburbs.'[176]

Such is also the opinion of the experts. It is what a report of the Council of Economic Analysis (CAE),[177] an organisation answering directly to the office of the Prime Minister, had shown in 2009. Entitled *Immigration, qualification et marché du travail (Immigration, Qualification, and the Labour Market)*, this document explains first of all that the notion of a 'labour shortage', traditionally alleged to justify the recourse to immigration, signifies almost nothing in a period of unemployment. 'From the point of view of economic science, the notion of a shortage is not evident', one may

---

[175] Michèle Tribalat, *Les yeux grands fermés: L'immigration en France* (Paris: Denoël, 2010).
[176] Philippe Nemo, online interview, *Le Temps d'y penser* site, 29 September 2010.
[177] Conseil d'analyse économique.—Ed.

read in the text, for the 'fact that certain locals reject certain types of work may simply signify that the workers have better opportunities than to take such jobs, and thus that the corresponding salaries should increase in order that they may be filled' (p. 45). Which clearly shows that shortage only occurs when a sector does not offer sufficient salaries — and that the recourse to immigration is in fact a means of not increasing salaries, even if it means artificially creating a 'shortage' that one will fill by going to look elsewhere for a workforce willing to be underpaid. The report concludes besides that, 'in the case of the labour market, that means that instead of the immigration of the 1960s, one could have envisaged a rise in the salary of the less qualified' (p. 46).

The same document lists a series of studies that, in France as well as abroad, have attempted to calculate the impact of immigration on salaries: 'Atlonji and Card find that a rise in the proportion of immigrants by 1% reduces the salary by 1.2%. ... Boris concludes his study by affirming that, between 1980 and 2000, immigration received work offers of around 11%, which would have reduced the salary of the locals by around 3.2%' (pp. 37–38).

Since the turn of the century, the annual intake of immigrants into the French population has been around 350,000 people, for the most part of non-European origin (of which 200,000 regular entries fall within the framework of professional immigration or of family reunification,[178] 50,000 asylum seekers, and 80,000 births of foreign origin). As the number of immigrants becoming French are increasing each year by almost 150,000, a good third of the French population should be derived from immigration by the middle of the century.

According to the official figures, immigrants living in an ordinary household today represent 5 million people, or 8% of the French population in 2008. The children of immigrants, direct descendants of one or two

---

[178] Family reunification is a policy which allows the family members of a foreign national who is residing in a European country to join him in that country. —Ed.

immigrants, represent 6.5 million persons, or 11% of the population. Illegal immigrants are estimated at between 300,000 and 550,000 people. (The expulsion of illegal immigrants costs 232 million euros a year, or 12,000 euros per repatriation.) Jean-Paul Gourévitch, for his part, estimates the population of foreign origin living in France in 2009 at 7.7 million people (of whom 3.4 million are Maghrebians and 2.4 million are of sub-Saharan origin), or 12.2% of the present metropolitan population. In 2006, this immigrant population contributed to 17% of the birth rate.

If immigration gives back to the private sector much more than it costs it, on the other hand it costs the public sector much more than it gives back to it.

The total cost of immigration has in fact been calculated. According to a study of the Taxpayers' Associated[179] prepared by Jean-Paul Gourévitch, *Le coût de la politique migratoire de la France (The Cost of Immigration Policy in France)*, the expenses that the state agrees to pay for immigration today amount to 79.4 billion euros a year, of which almost three-quarters (58.6 billion) come under social costs. As the receipts are rising to 48.9 billion euros, of which two-thirds are due to direct taxation (state and local governments) and to indirect taxes (VAT and the National Tax on Petroleum Products [TIPP]), the global deficit for public finances amounts to 30.4 billion euros, or 1.56% of the GDP. One will note that the *non-commercial* cost of immigration is not taken into consideration here. Gourévitch specifies that 'the studies conducted across the Channel and the Atlantic show that immigration does not have a globally positive effect on the public finances insofar as the immigration of settlers, which costs the state more than it gets back, remains higher in relation to the immigration of workforce, which gives back a little more than it costs when it is not illegal.'[180] He adds that if one adds to the deficits resulting from immigration also those which result from expatriation, or more than 11 billion euros of ex-

---

179 Contribuables Associés.—Ed.
180 Jean-Paul Gourévitch, 'La réalité de l'immigration', *La Nef*, May 2010, p. 14.

penses and loss of earnings for the state, 'the cost of the immigration policy of France is today established as being 38.3 billion euros, or almost 2% of the GDP.'[181]

France thus today experiences an immigration of settlers, a direct consequence of family reunification. But the immigrants constitute more than ever the reserve army of capital.

In this context, one can only be surprised to see how the illegal immigrant networks of the extreme Left, who believe that they have found a substitute proletariat in the immigrants, serve the interests of the employers. A mafia network, traffickers in men and merchandise, big bosses, 'humanitarian' militants, 'black market' employers: all are supporters of the abolition of borders through international free-tradeism. Olivier Besancenot,[182] Laurence Parisot,[183] same battle!

Revealing is the fact that Michael Hardt and Antonio Negri, in their manifesto books *Empire* and *Multitude*,[184] speak out for an 'international citizenship' and issue an appeal for the elimination of borders which would have as its first effect the acceleration of the installation in the developed countries of masses of low-wage workers coming from the Third World or emerging countries. That today the majority of immigrants owe their uprooting to the endless dislocations induced by the system of the global market, that this uprooting is precisely what capitalism seeks in order to better adapt men to the market, and finally, that attachment to one's territory is a part of the human psyche, does not in any way disturb these two authors. On the contrary, they note with satisfaction that '[c]apital itself has demanded the increased mobility of labor power and continuous migrations

---

181 *Ibid.*, p. 15.

182 Olivier Besancenot (b. 1974) is a French far-Left politician who ran for President in 2007. He is the main spokesman for the New Anticapitalist Party.—Ed.

183 Laurence Parisot (b. 1949) was head of the French MEDEF employers' union from 2005 until 2013, and is one of the wealthiest people in France.—Ed.

184 Michael Hardt and Antonio Negri, *Empire* (Cambridge, MA: Harvard University Press, 2000); *Multitude: War and Democracy in the Age of Empire* (New York: Penguin, 2004).

across national boundaries.'[185] The international market would constitute, in their view, the natural framework of 'international citizenship'. Because it 'requires a smooth space of uncoded and deterritorialized flows', the international market is supposed to serve the interests of the 'multitude', for '[t]he mobility does carry for capital a high price, however, which is the increased desire for liberation.'[186]

The problem with this apology for uprooting, taken as the precondition of a liberating 'nomadism', is that it is based on a totally unreal vision of the concrete situation of the immigrants and displaced persons. As Jacques Guigou and Jacques Wajnsztejn write, 'Hardt and Negri delude themselves regarding the capacity of the influx of immigrants to be at once the source of a new possibility for the development of capital as well as the basis of an improvement of the prospects for this multitude. Immigration is, in fact, nothing but a phase of a universal competition and, in itself, migrating is not any more liberating than remaining at home. The "nomadic" subject is no more inclined to criticism and revolt than the sedentary subject.'[187] 'So long', adds Robert Kurz, 'as men will leave their close relations and go, even at the risk of their lives, to seek work elsewhere — to be finally ground by the mill of capitalism — they will not be bearers of liberation any more than they will be the postmodern self-developers of the West: they only constitute the miserable variant of it.'[188]

One who criticises capitalism while approving of immigration, of which the working class is its first victim, would do better to remain silent.[189] One who criticises immigration while remaining silent regarding capitalism should do the same.

---

185 *Empire*, p. 400.

186 *Ibid.*, pp. 333 and 253.

187 Jacques Guigou and Jacques Wajnsztejn, *L'évanescence de la valeur: Une présentation critique du groupe Krisis* (Paris: L'Harmattan, 2004), p. 126.

188 Robert Kurz, 'L'Empire et ses théoriciens', in Anselm Jappe and Robert Kurz, *Les habits neufs de l'Empire: Remarques sur Negri, Hardt et Rufin* (Paris: Lignes-Léo-Scheer, 2003), pp. 114–115.

189 This is a paraphrase of a statement originally made by the Frankfurt School philosopher Max Horkheimer in 1939: 'Whoever is not prepared to talk about capitalism should also remain silent about fascism.'

Should a Citizenship Income Be Instituted?

'You wish to see the poor helped, I wish to see misery eliminated.'
—Victor Hugo, *Ninety-Three*

The global society has never been so rich as today. Would it not then be reasonable that rich societies distribute a part of their wealth to their citizens, even if it were only done from a perspective of 'social investment' to ensure a social cohesion that is threatened more than ever? After the creation of the SMIC[190] (Guaranteed Minimum Wage) in 1950, that of the RMI[191] (Minimum Integration Income) in 1988, and that of the RSA[192] (Social Welfare Allowance) in 2009, has the time not come, at a time when inequalities do not stop growing, to move from simple social aid to a radically new conception of economic solidarity? It is to these questions that the champions of a guaranteed social income reply in the affirmative.

It is given numerous names: 'citizenship income', 'social income', 'universal income', 'existence income', 'guaranteed income', 'autonomy income', 'universal allowance', 'social credit', 'dignity income', 'universal dividend', 'unconditional autonomy allowance', and so on. The term 'citizenship income' seems to be the best, for it has the merit of classifying the project within the framework of a polity, that is to say, of a given political com-

---

190 Salaire minimum interprofessionnel garanti.—Ed.
191 Revenu minimum d'insertion.—Ed.
192 Revenue de solidarité active.—Ed.

munity. Like the right to vote, the right to the citizenship income would follow from the mere fact of being a citizen.

The principle is the simplest one: it is a matter of paying a minimum income to each citizen from his birth to his death, which is unconditional, inalienable, equal for everyone, and cumulable, regardless of any other income or activity, and without any other tax reduction than that of the fiscal system in force. Contrary to the classic forms of minimum income (like the RMI, then the RSA), it is an income paid to all, poor and rich, on a strictly individual basis and without any demand for compensation (other than membership in a national community). The citizenship income thus manifests the political recognition of an unconditional right to the material survival of every citizen. It represents an act of solidarity which is exercised permanently, *a priori*, and no longer on demand and *a posteriori*. 'This revenue is granted because one exists and not for existing', says Yoland Bresson; it is 'a sort of "participation certificate" which sanctions a membership and engages the citizen in the community'.[193] Jean-Marc Ferry also defines it as a 'primary social income distributed equally in an unconditional way to the adult citizens of the major political community'. It is thus not at all a matter of 'monetarising' the citizenship — by definition citizenship does not have a price — but of adding a supplementary attribute to those that the citizens already have a prerogative to (certain of these attributes already having an economic or financial content). By its unconditionality, the citizenship income is distinguished from the social allowances that demand a search for work as a condition of receiving it. It cannot be withheld from the poorest, but enters into the tax base of the richest. It is a basic income that everyone supplements, or not, according to his needs.

The idea is not new. Plato already wrote in *The Laws*: 'We maintain that if a state is to avoid ... civil disintegration ... extreme poverty and wealth must not be allowed to arise in any section of the citizen-body.

---

[193] Yoland Bresson, 'Revenu d'existence et participat: vers la fin du salariat?', interview in *Krisis*, 18, November 1995, p. 68.

That is why the legislator must now announce the acceptable limits of wealth and poverty.'[194] In ancient Greece, the institution by Pericles of the *misthophoria*,[195] distributed to the citizens independently of their level of wealth in order that they may satisfy their civic obligations, already gives evidence 'of the demand for a universal solvency of the citizens superior to every other criterion as a factor of integration within the social group and of the capacity to exercise the rights and obligations which devolve upon them' (Janpier Dutrieux).

The idea of an unconditional income appeared in the sixteenth century from the pen of Thomas More (*Utopia*, 1516), but it seems indeed that it was the Spanish humanist Joan Lluís Vives who gave a coherent definition of it for the first time in his *De subventione pauperum* (1526). Two centuries later, the most cited example is that of Thomas Paine[196] who, in a manifesto on agrarian justice (*Agrarian Justice*) addressed to the Directory[197] in 1796 and published the following year, proposed that a sum of 15 pounds — with which one could buy a cow and a bit of land — be paid to all the young who have reached the age of majority, and that a uniform annual pension be paid to every person older than 50 years. This allowance was based on the idea of a common ownership of the land and on the sharing of a tax on land income. 'The first principle of civilisation', writes Paine, 'ought to have been and ought still to be, that the condition of every person born into the world, after a state of civilisation commences, ought not to be worse than if he had been born before that period.'[198] This unconditional allowance for every young person reaching the age of adulthood is the direct ancestor

---

194 Plato, *The Laws*, Book V, in *Plato: Complete Works* (Indianapolis: Hackett Publishing Company, 1997), p. 1425.—Ed.

195 The *misthophoria*, or paid function, was a salary paid to Athenian citizens who served in the courts as jurors.—Ed.

196 Thomas Paine (1737–1809) was an American political activist and philosopher whose writings were influential upon the American Revolution.—Ed.

197 The Directory was the national government of France from 1795 until 1799, during the French Revolution.—Ed.

198 Text that appeared in *La Revue du MAUSS*, 1st semester, 1996, p. 26.

of the citizenship income, the latter transposing to modern economies the project defended by Thomas Paine for the agrarian society of his time.

In the nineteenth century, Charles Fourier (1772–1837) declared that 'the first sign of justice should be to guarantee to the people a minimum that grows on account of social progress.' This idea of a basic income for all is found also in the *Solution du problème social* of the Brussels Fourierist,[199] Joseph Charlier, published in 1848.

At the beginning of the 1930s, Jacques Duboin (1878–1976), theoretician of 'abundancism', defined the 'social income' (an expression that he was the first to employ) as the materialisation of a new freedom opening access to the sphere of non-market values. Elected deputy of Haute-Savoie in 1922, and under-secretary of state to the treasury in 1924, his distributive theory, propounded in numerous works,[200] envisages at the same time a guaranteed existence income 'from the cradle to the grave' and the institution of a currency secured on production. He counted Jean Weiland and Jacques Sarrazin among his disciples.

In monetary matters, Duboin maintained theses quite close to the theory of 'free money'[201] developed in 1916 by the German Silvio Gesell (1862–1930), who wished to burden the currency with a rate of depreciation in order to promote its circulation and prevent its hoarding. The point of departure in his reasoning rests on his assessment that the classic use of currency prohibits the balancing of distributed incomes with the wealth that is put on the market, which has as its result the establishment of 'misery in abundance'. 'It should therefore be replaced by a currency created for this sole purpose. That could be done ... starting from the principle that every citizen has the right to receive sufficient incomes for life provided that he fulfils, for a part of the time, a duty of participation, the whole be-

---

199 Fourierism was a form of utopian socialism based on communitarian principles, formulated by Charles Fourier in the early nineteenth century.—Ed.

200 Cf., in particular, Jacques Duboin, *Kou l'ahuri, la misère dans l'abondance* (1931), *La grande relève des hommes par la machine* (1932), and *Demain ou le socialisme de l'abondance* (1944).

201 *Freigeld* (Fr. *monnaie franche* or *monnaie fondante*), etc.—Ed.

ing managed through the intermediary of a consumption currency staked on the available wealth. ... The capitalist currency should be substituted by a currency created as and when wealth is produced, proportionately to it, through the intermediary of politically defined prices, and annulled as and when it is sold to be consumed. This consumption currency is a purchasing power which serves only once: it does not circulate and cannot produce any interests. But it remains the ballot of the client for the production that is to be renewed, since it keeps its full freedom to choose its purchases.'[202] In this system, the amount of monetary supply issued during a given period equals the total price of the goods put on sale in the same period of time. To every new production corresponds the issuing of a new quantity of currency. A part of this sum is allocated to public services, the rest being distributed among the citizens.

One finds similar ideas in the work of the Scot, C H Douglas (1879–1952), founder of the school of 'social credit'. Douglas was convinced that the nature of industrial production, combined with the monopoly of monetary creation held by the banking system, has as its effect the creation of situations of artificial shortage for the majority of the population. Money, for him, should be, not a measure of value, but a symbol of value, whose volume of circulation should increase and decrease in strict proportion to increases and decreases of the corresponding goods. The currency should be distributed to the citizens in the form of dividends.[203]

Analogous theories were also held during the inter-war period by the personalists and federalists of the journal *L'Ordre nouveau* (Alexandre Marc),[204] who stood for a 'social minimum', and by Gustave Rodrigues, a

---

[202] Marie-Louise Duboin, 'L'économie distributive', *Agone*, 21, 1999, pp. 120 and 132. Resumed by his daughter, the journal *La Grande Relève*, founded in October 1935 by Jacques Duboin, still appears today (B.P. 108, 78115 Le Vésinet Cédex).

[203] Cf. C H Douglas, *Economic Democracy* (Sudbury: Bloomfield Books, 1974). On 'social credit' and 'economic democracy', cf. the journal *The Social Crediter* managed by Frances Hutchinson (PO Box 322, Silsden, Keighley, West Yorkshire, BD20 0YE, Great Britain).

[204] Alexandre Marc (1904–2000) was a French philosopher who founded a Personalist integral federalist current of thought. His thought was influential on the French New Right. See John Hellman, *Communitarian Third Way: Alexandre Marc and Ordre Nouveau, 1930–2000* (Montreal: McGill-Queen's University Press, 2002).—Ed.

close associate of Georges Valois[205] who committed suicide in Bordeaux in 1940.[206] Valois himself was inspired by it in the formulation of his 'Plan of the New Age' (17 February 1936), which was communalist and cooperative in spirit.

At the end of the 1950s, a proposal of fiscal reform was presented to the National Assembly by Jean-Pierre Parrot, deputy for Allier, in which he suggested the creation of a single national payment for all Frenchmen. This initiative did not have any result. The idea of a citizenship income seemed then to be clearly related to utopia, which did not however prevent it from being defended by personalities as diverse as Bertrand Russell, John Kenneth Galbraith, Jan Tinbergen, James Tobin, Paul Samuelson, Sicco Mansholt, and others. But it was especially from the beginning of the 1980s that one saw it resurge strongly, the most remarkable fact being that personalities coming from the most diverse backgrounds slowly began rallying to it.

The principle of a guaranteed social income has thus been successively defended by Yann Moulier-Boutang, the present editor of the journal *Multitudes*;[207] by the journal *Cash*, which is an organ of the Association of the Unemployed and the Professionally Insecure (ACP);[208] by the Agitation Committee for an Optimal Guaranteed Income (Cargo)[209] of Laurent Guilloteau; by the network *No Pasaran*; by the libertarian journal *La Griffe*, but also by the MAUSS[210] of Alain Caillé; by Jacques Robin and Patrick Viveret during the time of the journal *Transversales Science/Culture*; by several ecological movements; and by the Gaullist Yoland Bresson.

---

205 Georges Valois (1878–1945) was a French journalist and politician. Originally an anarcho-syndicalist in Georges Sorel's circle, and later joined the Action Française of Charles Maurras. In 1911 he formed the Cercle Proudhon, which attempted to merge Maurras' Integralism with Sorel's syndicalism, and is seen by some as a prefiguration of fascism. Joining the French Resistance during the occupation, he died in Bergen-Belsen.—Ed.

206 Gustave Rodrigues, *Le droit à la vie* (Paris: Liberté, 1934).

207 Cf. Yann Moulier-Boutang, 'L'autre globalisation: le revenu d'existence inconditionnel, individuel et substantiel', *Multitudes*, 8, 2002.

208 Association des chômeurs et des précaires.—Ed.

209 Comité pour un revenu garanti optimal.—Ed.

210 Mouvement anti-utilitariste dans les sciences sociales.—Ed.

Some years ago, Christine Boutin, President of the Christian Democratic party and former housing minister, herself rallied to the idea of a 'universal dividend' inspired by social Catholicism. In 2009, finally, Olivier Auber launched an 'Appeal for a Life Income'.

The existence income also has partisans among liberals, but these understand it in a very particular form — which should not deceive us. It is in this way that the American economist Milton Friedman, reviving an idea that had already been advanced in the 1940s by the Englishwoman Juliet Rhys-Williams, spoke out for a minimum income taking the form of a 'negative tax credit' in 1962, for the sole purpose of rendering unemployment and job precariousness more tolerable. It was a matter of a simple refundable tax credit calculated at the level of the household (instead of being an individual allowance) which would be paid to non-taxable families and would function, for those eligible to pay tax, as a classic tax reduction.[211] More recently, the libertarian Charles Murray also proposed to convert all social transfer payments into a single allowance, fixed and uniform for all citizens.[212] The same solution is today advocated in France by the 'Alternatives libérales'[213] movement. The existence income, in this view, obviously has nothing more to do with the distribution of incomes but is equivalent to a disguised subsidy to businesses. The idea is to grant a guaranteed income in exchange for the freedom for employers to set salaries outside all legal constraints, which comes down to abolishing established conventions and all regulation of the labour market. The negative tax in fact constitutes a system for subsidising low salaries, which invites businesses to use and abuse the job 'flexibility' and to lower the wages they offer, which is exactly the opposite of the objective of the citizenship income.[214]

---

211 Cf. Milton Friedman, *Capitalism and Freedom* (Chicago: University of Chicago Press, 1962).

212 Cf. Charles Murray, *In Our Hands: A Plan to Replace the Welfare State* (Washington, DC: AEI Press, 2006).

213 Liberal Alternative is a political party founded in 2006. It stands for classical liberalism as opposed to either socialism or conservatism.—Ed.

214 In the 1960s, a negative tax was tested as an experiment in New Jersey in the United States, in which 30,000 families benefited from it for three years. This showed that this measure clearly favours 'black market' work.

The principal theoreticians of the existence income today are Philippe Van Parijs, holder of the Hoover Chair of Economic and Social Ethics at the Université de Louvain-La-Neuve, Jean-Marc Ferry, and Yoland Bresson,[215] and also André Gorz and René Passet. Van Parijs created the network BIEN (Basic Income European Network, rechristened Basic Income Earth Network in 2004) in 1986, which publishes the journal *Basic Income Studies* and of which he is the General Secretary. In France, the Association for the Establishment of an Existence Income (AIRE),[216] founded by the economist Henri Guitton and affiliated with the BIEN network, popularises the theses of Yoland Bresson.[217]

A start in the practical application of this idea has also begun in certain countries. In Alaska in the United States, every citizen annually receives a share (modest, but allotted unconditionally) of the petrol revenues of this state. A basic income for aged persons was established in Bolivia in 2008. In Brazil, the government gave a green light in 2004 to the progressive establishment of an existence income. In Great Britain, the workers[218] have introduced an allowance for each newborn, untouchable until the age of majority, but which collects compound interest up to that age.

But it is above all the rise of unemployment which explains the dramatic return of the idea of a citizenship income. For more than 30 years mass unemployment that nothing seems capable of stopping has been developing in the rich countries, since it continues to grow in all the industrialised countries, whatever the policies maintained in them may be. By virtue of

---

215 Cf. Philippe Van Parijs, *Arguing for Basic Income* (London: Verso, 1992); *Real Freedom for All: What (If Anything) Can Justify Capitalism?* (Oxford: Clarendon Press, 1995); *Refonder la solidarité* (Paris: Cerf, 1996); Jean-Marc Ferry, *L'allocation universelle: Pour un revenu de citoyenneté* (Paris: Cerf, 1996); Yoland Bresson, *L'après-salariat: Une nouvelle approche de l'économie* (Economica, Paris, 1993). Cf. also Gilles Gantelet and Jean-Paul Maréchal (eds.), *Garantir le revenue: Une des solutions à l'exclusion* (Paris: Transversales Science/Culture, 1992); François Blais, *Un revenu garanti pour tous: Introduction aux principes de l'allocation universelle* (Montreal: Boréal, 2001); and Baptiste Mylondo, *Ne pars perdre sa vie à la gagner: Pour un revenu de citoyenneté* (Paris: Homnisphères, 2008).

216 Association pour l'instauration d'un revenu d'existence.—Ed.

217 She also publishes a quarterly bulletin, *La Lettre de l'AIRE* (33 avenue des Fauvettes, 91440 Bures-s/Yvette).

218 In French, *travaillistes*, or members of the Labour Party.—Ed.

gains in productivity, innovation is no longer automatically a creator of jobs. Work is becoming rare. That is not to say that it is going to disappear, as Jeremy Rifkin imprudently prognosticated in the 1990s,[219] but that, on account of automation, computerisation, and robotisation, ever more goods and services are produced with ever fewer hours of human work, and finally with ever fewer men. In spite of demographic growth, international production per inhabitant has multiplied 2.5 times between 1960 and 1990. This level of production has been achieved with an ever smaller recourse to human labour, for which reason the total number of hours worked has not stopped diminishing in almost all the developed countries. Certain economists even envisage a time when 20% of the world's potentially working population could suffice to produce all the goods and services which the globalised society would need. The era of full-time employment thus seems to be at an end: 'The illusion of a salaried and duly remunerated job for all evaporated with the crisis' (Olivier Auber). Its consequence of is that the distribution of wealth according to work does not stop decreasing and the protection of the unemployed (or the unemployable) becomes ever heavier. In such conditions, the system must sooner or later come up against internal limits.

'Growth no longer creates employment', explains Yoland Bresson, 'because the positive effects that it exercised before in this field are now annulled by continual gains in productivity. However, the governments that have followed one another in the last decades have not stopped treating unemployment like a passing accident which should be dealt with while waiting for the return of full employment. They have thus privileged the social welfare treatment of unemployment and assistance, whose financing has continued to be provided mostly by those holding salaried jobs. As the number of the latter is continually shrinking, one has entered into a vicious

---

219 Jeremy Rifkin (b. 1945) published a book, *The End of Work*, in 1995 in which he predicted that innovations in technology would render the need for most forms of human labour obsolete. He postulated that voluntary and community-based initiatives would take its place that would provide more social services.—Ed.

circle.'²²⁰ 'Jobs are running out', likewise observes Gilles Yovan, 'even if society does not want to hear about a crisis of the wage-earning system and rejects the evidence, preferring to attribute the persistence of mass unemployment in the European countries to conjecture.'²²¹

The moment one succeeds in producing more and more goods with fewer and fewer men, the essential problem ceases to be that of production and becomes that of distribution. Under such conditions, it is in fact a matter of knowing how an ever-growing volume of merchandise could be absorbed while one simultaneously observes a global reduction in purchasing power — the sale capacity continuing to grow while purchasing capacity diminishes. If this problem is not resolved, unemployment continues to increase at the same time as production, and growth mechanically enlarges the gap between the richest and the poorest.

But this development, if it negatively results in unemployment and job precariousness, also potentially bears the hope of a progressive emancipation of salaried work and of the phenomena of worker exploitation that are linked to it. It is in fact necessary to understand clearly that a machine that replaces a man eliminates a job, and thus a salary, but not the work to be done. It is thus not work that becomes rarer, but employment. The generalisation of this phenomenon could facilitate the establishment of a citizenship income. 'In a context of a reduction of employment', writes Jean Zin, 'one of two things follows: either social protections are attached to the job, with the consequences of inequality and exclusion that we know especially from the fact that work is becoming erratic and precarious, or social protections are attached to the *person*, and that should result, at least, in a guaranteed income.'²²²

One would thus pass from a redistributive economy to a *distributive* economy (also called an 'economy of needs'). 'The redistribution of wealth

---

220 'Revenu d'existence et participat', *art. cit.*, p. 68.

221 Gilles Yovan, debate: 'Le revenu social: sortir de la société salariale', online text, *Productions. Les périphériques vous parlent* site.

222 Jean Zin, 'Vers la révolution du revenu garanti?', online text, 5 April 2006.

through the intermediary of work', emphasises Marie-Louise Duboin, 'does not offer the means of preventing the diminution of the purchasing power of a growing part of the population to the advantage of the greatest fortunes. It is thus necessary to replace this redistribution by work with the distribution of the wealth produced, when it is produced with increasingly less work.'[223]

For those who support its principle, the establishment of a citizenship income would have multiple advantages. Such an income 'would permit at the same time the eradication of poverty, the elimination of unemployment, the reduction of inequalities and social injustices, and the emancipation of the individual', exclaims Baptiste Mylondo in an almost lyrical outburst.[224] The establishment of an existence income being an evident factor favouring social integration, it would in any case allow for the struggle against exclusion, which has not stopped increasing in spite of the explosion of social transfers. Mathematically, it would besides bring about an increase in purchasing power, at the same time as a reduction of income gaps. Favouring autonomy, it would allow new arbitrations between work time and free time. It would not be stigmatising since, 'contrary to help given on condition of possessing certain resources, the beneficiaries would not have to give proof of their poverty. In other words, the fact of receiving existence revenue would not be synonymous with any state of marginalisation whatsoever.'[225] Being unconditionally distributed to all, the citizenship income likewise avoids all political wrangling and does not encourage fraud, contrarily to the majority of social allowances. It is also of a kind that causes the relationship between the wage-earners and the employers to develop, the former no longer being in a situation of needing to accept any job merely to survive (the less one needs to earn money, the less one will be inclined to accept badly paid and degrading jobs). By helping to make the

---

223 'L'économie distributive', *art. cit.*, p. 129.

224 Baptiste Mylondo, *Un revenu pour tous! Précis d'utopie réaliste* (Paris: Utopia, 2010), p. 7.

225 Jean-Paul Maréchal, *Humaniser l'économie* (Paris: Desclée de Brouwer, 2008).

transition between two periods of wage-earnings, it would allow one to bear the wait and its associated costs more effectively. It should also permit savings by reducing the administrative costs of the present system of social allowance.

Philippe Van Parijs sees in it a 'soft technique of work-sharing', Yann Moulier-Boutang the 'recognition of the collective social character of the creation of wealth'. 'The level of production of a company ... incorporates the historical contribution of preceding generations', writes Alain Caillé for his part. 'Henceforth the distribution of an existence income makes manifest the share of the production that objectively derives from this common heritage.' Finally, the citizenship income can be paid to minors in a blocked account. 'On reaching his age of majority', Yoland Bresson remarks, 'a child who will have received the existence revenue since his birth will be able to make use of a certain amount of monetary capital which will permit him to make choices; pursue his studies, travel, realise a personal productive project allowing him to integrate into society, etc.'[226]

However, the principal advantage of the citizenship income is obviously that it would be of a kind that would challenge salaried work as the basis of capital and its social relations. By helping to escape from the framework of the generalised wage-earning system and by creating a sort of alternative to salaried work, it would prevent the latter from colonising all the spheres of existence, contradicting at the same time the idea, which is spread by employers as well as by the ruling ideology, that salaried work is the only possible basis of society, the only source of social cohesion, and that, without it, one cannot live 'with dignity'. 'In a very visible way', emphasises Philippe Van Parijs, 'a much more important share of the income of the citizens would be distributed to them by the state as citizens, and a clearly much less important share by their employers as salaried workers.'[227]

---

226 *Art. cit.*, p. 69.
227 Philippe Van Parijs, interview in *Multitudes*, April 2002.

With the citizenship income, salaried work ceases to be the only possible mode of social inclusion, and even of socialisation.

In his books on the *Métamorphoses du travail*[228] and on *L'immatériel*,[229] André Gorz, who, at the end of his life, rallied to the citizenship income after having been hostile to it for a long time,[230] opposes 'self-production' to forced work, which he qualifies as 'heteronomous'. The latter has only an instrumental value for the individual; corresponding to an exchange value, it does not have meaning in itself — that is to say, it does not deserve to be undertaken in itself, but derives its sole *raison d'être* from the income that it allows one to obtain and from the symbolic privilege that society confers on all those who work. Work as 'self-production' is, on the contrary, work which makes sense for the individual: it is the 'living labour' that expresses the development of the capacities due to which the individual can produce himself as an individual subject.[231] Now, 'those holding economic and political power', recalls André Gorz, 'fear above all one thing: that the time outside salaried work can become the dominant time from the social and cultural point of view, and that the people may decide to take this time to employ themselves. ... Capitalism ensures that the people consider themselves as being only a workforce on a labour market, and that, if they do not find an employer, they have only themselves to blame for it, that is to say, for the fact that they are not sufficiently "employable."'[232]

But the production of oneself cannot be limited to the sphere of leisure time activities or hobbies, that is to say, to the field of consumption. Society should allow the deployment of autonomous activities, detached from the salarial relationship, in the field of production itself. It has therefore as a

---

228 *Métamorphoses du travail: Critique de la raison économique* (*Metamorphoses of Work*) (Paris: Galilée, 1988).—Ed.

229 *L'immatériel: Connaissance, valeur et capital* (*The Immaterial*) (Paris: Galilée, 2003).—Ed.

230 Until 1997, he considered it as a guaranteed, but conditional, social income. Cf. André Gorz, *Reclaiming Work: Beyond the Wage-Based Society* (Cambridge, UK: Blackwell, 1999); 'Qui ne travaille pas ne mangera pas quand même', *Futuribles*, July–August 1986, pp. 56–74.

231 Cf. Gilles Yovan, 'La production de soi dans le cadre du capitalisme de l'immatériel', online text, *Productions: Les périphériques vous parlent* site.

232 André Gorz, 'Oser l'exode of the work society', 'Les périphériques vous parlent', Spring 1998.

condition going beyond, if not the salaried society itself, at least an exclusively salarial relationship at work. This is what the citizenship income can contribute to, by allowing one to move from *suffered* work to *chosen* work. For Jean Zin, who sees in it a means of 'changing work in order to change life', the citizenship income constitutes 'a considerable social progress of our autonomy favouring an exit from salaried capitalism for the benefit of autonomous work, as well as a relocalised economy integrating the ecological dimension and oriented towards human development. ... The guaranteed income is the institution permitting the passage from forced work to chosen work in a more cooperative and convivial society.'[233]

To act in such a way that the existence of individuals ceases to depend solely on the sale of oneself as a labour force, and that salaried work is not the sole source of social status, implies in fact a double disconnection. It is a matter, first, of disconnecting work from income, but also of disconnecting work from employment, the reduction of the former to the latter ending in the exclusion of those who are deprived of employment, in fear of unemployment among the salaried workers, and in the subjection of those who require help to social control. Here again, it is very important not to confuse work and employment. 'Employment is only work turned into merchandise, contractually subjected to the authority and the demands of an employer, and whose price is determined by the market.'[234] The citizenship income takes the opposing view of the dominant idea in this respect, that 'the struggle against poverty passes through employment' (Martin Hirsch). Poverty is first, in fact a matter of income. The citizenship income represents a change in the distribution of incomes and not, like the RSA,[235] a new allocation of redistributive assistance being added to the others. The centrality of salaried work derives today from the fact of its permitting sub-

---

[233] Jean Zin, 'Pour un New Deal: revenu garanti pour tous', online text, 16 October 2008.
[234] Yoland Bresson, 'RSA ou revenu d'existence', *La Lettre de l'AIRE*, 57, Summer 2008.
[235] Revenue de solidarité active (Work-solidarity Income)—the French social welfare allowance.—Ed.

sistence. One can even see in it a 'subsistence blackmail'.[236] But in reality it is subsistence itself which should become central, not work.

The establishment of the citizenship income could finally be accompanied by a certain number of other initiatives. It is thus that, for André Gorz, the allocation of a social income is 'inseparable from the development and accessibility of the means permitting and encouraging self-activity'. Among these means are also included the 'cooperative circles', the local currencies, and the local exchange trading systems (SEL)[237] as well as the 'municipal cooperatives' whose creation Jean Zin proposes, inspired by the theses of Murray Bookchin, theoretician of social ecology and of 'libertarian municipalism'. Others simply confide in associative activities, sometimes with a certain naivety, for it is doubtful if they can overcome the secular contradictions between the historical dynamic and the capitalist system and the wage-earning institutions by themselves.

If the advantages have been strongly emphasised, there are also numerous objections opposed to the idea of citizenship income. Some are moral objections, others economic objections. Some point to the principle of citizenship income itself, many concern its feasibility, in particular its financing. Still others have a more general scope. It is these objections that we are now going to review.

The moral criticism is generally based on the old Christian idea according to which work constitutes the obligatory fate of humanity since the original sin ('he who does not work does not eat,' said St Paul). Man is destined by nature to earn his living 'by the sweat of his brow'. This idea has inspired all the justifications of work that have been seen to flourish, on the Right as well as on the Left, on the subject of the 'work ethic', of the 'dignity of labour', and of the 'right to work', denounced in its time by

---

236 *Sortir de l'économie*, 2 May 2008, p. 41.

237 The local exchange trading systems (Systèmes d'échanges locaux, SEL) have already created currencies with time-limited validity which can therefore not be capitalised since the 1990s. The objective is to reinvest currency with a social character (cf. *Alternatives économiques*, 157, March 1998).

Paul Lafargue.[238] It is implicitly present in the manner in which, even today, the parties of the Right develop an unconditional and unlimited conception of labour value. In their view, 'working is a categorical imperative, for, apart from the fact that it is necessary for the production of wealth, work accomplishes the moral demand of not becoming or remaining a social welfare dependent' (Robert Castel). It is also the basis of the denunciation by liberals of the 'voluntarily unemployed' and other work-dodgers, who are viewed basically as social parasites, a critique which suggests that mass unemployment would disappear if everybody accepted to work under no matter what conditions.[239] 'France should not be a leisure park', said Jean-Pierre Raffarin in 2003. Some years later, one remembers the slogan of Nicolas Sarkozy during his 2007 presidential campaign: 'Work more to earn more.' But earn more to do what? To consume more, of course.[240]

One also finds this moral critique in the idea that the establishment of the citizenship income would come down to encouraging laziness and remunerating laziness. The error lies in the assimilation of all forms of human activity to 'work', and more specifically to salaried work. Rather, to refuse salaried work is not to want to 'do nothing'. If one understands work in the sense of doing, realising, acting, and creating, work will never disappear. Salaried work itself has, for a long time, been perceived as a form of slavery (half a century ago, the abolition of the wage-earning system still figured in

---

238 Paul Lafargue (1842–1911) was a French revolutionary socialist, and was Marx's son-in-law. In 1880 he published a book, *The Right to be Lazy*, in which he argued that the 'right to work' was tantamount to enslavement, and held that laziness was vital to progress. The book is available online at www.marxists.org/archive/lafargue/1883/lazy/.—Ed.

239 Let us emphasise however that the presence of a relatively high rate of unemployment does not go against the interests of capital, but indeed the opposite. When unemployment is not very high, the workers are more demanding about their salaries and their conditions of work, for they know they will not have difficulty in finding a job if they decide to leave what they already have. When unemployment is very high, they are in turn ready to accept no matter what job in order to avoid unemployment. Cf. David Schweickart, *After Capitalism* (Lanham, MD: Rowman and Littlefield, 2002).

240 The countries that have the highest rates of employment are, in reality, those where the duration of work is the shortest. Let us remember also that, in France, the businesses that switched to 35 hours per week registered a rise of 6.7% in their hourly productivity for a lowering of work-time of around 10%, between 1997 and 2000. From this point of view, 'working more' signifies the opposite of 'everybody working'. Cf. Brieuc Bougnoux, 'Travailler plus ne permet pas de gagner plus', *Alternatives économiques*, 263, November 2007.

the programme of the CGT).[241] We should remember here the distinction that the Greeks made between drudgery (*ponos*) and creative work (*poiesis*), the latter being the sole vector of self-realisation. This distinction is also found in the thought of Hegel and Marx (who advocated the transformation of work into 'self-activity').

We should also remember that capitalism is the social form which 'could develop only by abstracting work from the person who does it, his intention, his needs, to define him in himself as an expense of measurable energy, exchangeable for any other form of it, and whose providers, the "workers", are in many respects interchangeable. The "abstract work" invented by capitalism is merchandise that the employer buys and whose purpose, content, hours, and price he determines arbitrarily. ... The wage-earning system is thus the complete dispossession of the working person: he is dispossessed of the result or product of his activity, of the use of his time, of the choice in the purposes and contents of the work, and of the means of work that the employers, at the end of the eighteenth century, began to monopolise to be able to force the people — the weavers first of all — to work for an employer and to kill all possibility of self-production, of self-activity.'[242]

The fear of seeing a society of idle and lazy people establish itself along with the citizenship income seems vain. The establishment of this income will not at all bring about a massive decline in participation in the labour market, but would rather free everyone from the obligation of finding a job at no matter what price, which would oblige employers to offer better conditions for numerous jobs. It is much rather the present unemployment allowances which often dissuade people from looking for work, since they are diminished or abolished when the work incomes increase. The citizenship income does not encourage one not to work anymore, since one receives it even when working. The simulation models which have been presented in

---

241 Confédération Générale du Travail, the French Labour Union.—Ed.
242 André Gorz, '"Oser l'exode" de la société de travail', *art. cit.* p. 44.

the different congresses of the BIEN envisage, besides, only a reduction of work of weak amplitude on the part of the badly-paid workers. The experiments conducted between 1968 and 1980 in the United States also belie the hypothesis of a massive desertion of the labour market in the case of the establishment of a citizenship income. André Gorz has himself insisted vociferously on the idea that the guaranteed income does not at all have as its objective the exemption from work but, much rather, the granting of better means for choosing one's work. Similarly Jean Zin: 'The guaranteed income is not destined to pay people for doing nothing, but to give them more autonomy in the choice of their activity.'

The criticism according to which the citizenship income would transform all citizens into welfare dependants, thus reinforcing the idea that to be a citizen is above all to be a claimant, is no longer acceptable: 'The existence income is not a charity, for, once provided with necessities, the individual experiences the need to act and to realise himself.'[243]

Another argument is that the creation of an existence income would constitute a new 'suction effect' favouring immigration. The response to this argument is that, to the extent that it would substitute the majority of the present allowances, this measure could also contribute to curbing them. The guaranteed income being reserved for the citizens, one could thus envisage that the establishment of the citizenship income would go hand-in-hand with a revision of the conditions by which nationality is attributed. 'The status of citizen', estimates Yoland Bresson, 'should be acquired only under certain conditions, notably that of a sufficient integration into French society and of a participation in French exchange times.'[244]

But the most common objection obviously concerns the feasibility of the project. Is the citizenship income viable from the economic and financial point of view? And where does one find one's financing?

---

[243] Louis Lievin, *La Lettre de l'AIRE*, Spring 2008, p. 9.

[244] 'Revenu d'existence et participat,' *art. cit.*, p. 75. ('Exchange time' is paid time off from work in exchange for overtime work.—Ed.)

The response clearly depends on the level of this income. It is already necessary that this level be sufficient for living, even if modestly, failing which the citizenship income would at once be useless for the rich and derisory for the most impoverished. It appears difficult, for example, to eliminate the RSA by replacing it with a basic income whose amount would be lower. But the citizenship income should also be compatible with what is economically and financially possible taking into consideration the budget of the state. Its amount, finally, should be indexed on inflation (but it must be noted that it is not inflationary, since it follows the development of the national revenue).

Much ambiguity is attached to the fact that, for some (André Gorz), the citizenship income must be sufficient only for that person who would be content to live on it, whereas, for others (Yoland Bresson, Philippe Van Parijs), it is a matter only of a basic income that should be necessarily combined with other incomes. André Gorz wished that it be fixed at the level of the Smic.[245] Among the Greens, Yves Cochet fights for an 'unconditional minimum income' of 600 euros per month. Jean Zin speaks of an amount of 750 euros. The creation of an income of 817 euros per adult was also envisaged in 2009 in the Europe Écologie programme.[246] In the United States, Richard C Cook thinks that an annual income of around 12,600 dollars could be ensured to all citizens. A number of these proposals take as their point of reference the poverty line (fixed in France at 60% of the median income).

As for the question of financing, it should first of all be well formulated. 'The problem posed by the existence income is not that of the amount or the mass of necessary resources for it', emphasises Yoland Bresson, 'since its level depends precisely on this amount, but solely that of its distribution. Let us take for example four card players. Instead of distributing the

---

245 Minimum wage.—Ed.

246 Europe Ecology is a coalition of Green parties that formed in 2008. It has contested the European parliamentary elections in 2009 and 2014, and has met with some success.—Ed.

52 playing cards at random, one first gives one ace to each of the players, and then one distributes the remaining 48 cards at random. The number of playing cards has not changed, it is the manner of distributing them that has changed. Who loses in this new distribution? The extremes: the champion, who will have henceforth to deal with players possessing at least one good card, exactly like the employer who will offer a job to a job-seeker encouraged by his existence income to make his choices more carefully, and, on the other hand, the bad players, who will no longer be able to impute their successive mistakes to bad luck alone. The establishment of an existence income comes down, similarly, to a simple problem of the distribution of existing wealth.'[247]

In the estimates that have been made, the source of financing most often proposed is to transfer a part of the funds that are today allocated for social welfare. In the system of citizenship income, the latter do not have the same *raisons d'être* any longer. The citizenship income would replace the majority of the present redistributive mechanisms and social aids (API,[248] RSA, social minimums, family allowances, housing allowance, family-quotient taxation,[249] supplementary family allowance,[250] job bonuses, tax exemptions, social pricing policies, agricultural subsidies, etc.), excepting social security (which is an insurance and not an allowance), unemployment insurance, certain housing benefits, and allowances for the handicapped. It should be recalled here that, according to the INSEE, the social allowances represent in themselves 44.1% of the public expense, or 437 billion euros in 2007.[251] From this total, the amount of sums redistributed exceeds 337 billion euros per year, of which a total of 288 billion could be allocated to the citizenship income. The rest of the financing would be ensured by the

---

[247] *Ibid.*, p. 72.
[248] Allocation de parent isolé (Single parent allowance).—Ed.
[249] In France the family, rather than the individual, is the entity that is subject to taxation.—Ed.
[250] Supplément familial de traitement (SFT).—Ed.
[251] The relative share of social allowances in the household incomes had already passed from 22% in 1970 to nearly 33% in 1997.

elimination of a certain number of tax loopholes and by a reform of direct and indirect taxation, providing for, in particular, the elimination of tax brackets and their replacement by a simple system of linear progressivity from the first euro received.

Yoland Bresson has presented a plan for financing the existence revenue based on an allocation of 300 euros monthly.[252] This figure corresponds to a total annual allocation of 216 billion euros for 60 million people, a figure tderived from a GDP of 1,500 billion euros. The amount would be fixed at the beginning within the framework of a social programme act, and then readjusted each year contingent on the national product. A transitory phase of five years is provided for, allowing the progressive passage from the wage-earning system to the 'participation' system. During this transition period, Bresson proposes borrowing from the banking sector at a real interest rate of 1% a year, but with an as it were unlimited deadline in the form of a perpetual allowance. For the additional financing he envisages recourse to borrowing from the state on savings.

Christine Boutin also asks for the introduction of a dividend of a monthly amount of 330 euros. The Modelling a Universal Allowance in France (MAUF)[253] proposed by Marc de Basquiat provides for the removal of a uniform tax on income at the present maximum rate, and the sharing of the sums redistributed today in diverse ways through an allocation distributed to each citizen in the form of a negative monthly tax, or a basic income of 385 euros for adults. Others, we have seen, wish for a higher allocation. The Vivant-Europe movement[254] has taken a stand for a basic income adjusted according to age (150 euros up to 17 years, 444 euros from 18 to 24 years, 600 euros from 25 to 64 years). The liberal Jacques Marseille

---

252 *La Lettre de l'AIRE*, 62, Autumn 2009, pp. 20–21; *Le partage du temps et des revenus* (Paris: Economica, 1994), pp. 91–95. Cf. also Marc de Basquiat's paper 'Rationalisation d'un système distributif complexe: la piste de l'allocation universelle', presented in September 2009 at the 29th Journées de l'Association d'économie sociale (*La Lettre de l'AIRE*, 64, Spring 2010).

253 Modélisation de l'allocation universelle en France. —Ed.

254 Vivant-Europe proposes to eliminate taxes on work in the European Union, and a 'social VAT' on the sale of products in Europe in order to fund social security. See their Website at vivant-europe.eu/home.

has spoken out for a monthly allocation of 750 euros for adults and 375 for minors, this allocation replacing all others, including pensions.[255] René Passet fixes the basic income at the level of the poverty line (around 950 euros per month) for adults and at half of this amount for those younger than 20 years.[256] This plan corresponds to a total allocation of 470 billion per year, or almost a third of the GDP.

Some authors, like André Gorz, think that the social income should not take the form of a classic capital, but that of a different currency, such as the 'consumption currency' of which Jacques Duboin spoke. In this system, every market product is automatically accompanied by the issue of its 'monetary equivalent', that is to say, by a quantity of consumption currency allowing the purchase of the goods produced. The currency issued in this way could serve only once: it would be automatically annulled at the moment of purchase. This system is quite comparable to the 'social credit' of C H Douglas or the 'free money' of Silvio Gesell, which was mentioned above. However, it poses problems of which André Gorz is very aware: 'How does one establish the monetary equivalent of a product at the moment of its production, especially when this production demands only very little work? Its exchange value, its price, cannot be determined by the market, since the issue of consumption currency should take place before or at the moment of its being placed on the market. For the quantity of currency issued to correspond to the sale price, the prices should be fixed *ex ante*[257] by a "citizen's contract" between consumers, businessmen, and public powers. It is necessary, in other words, that the prices be political prices, and that the price system be the reflection of a political choice; that is of a choice of the society concerning the model of consumption and the priorities that the society wishes to give itself.'[258]

---

255 Jacques Marseille, *L'argent des Français* (Paris: Perrin, 2008).
256 René Passet, *L'illusion néolibérale* (Paris: Fayard, 2000), pp. 274–275.
257 Latin: 'before the event'.—Ed.
258 *Mouvements*, June 2007.

Other critiques, sometimes very sharp, have also been issued against citizenship income. Some of them deserve to be considered.

One can first ask oneself if there is really any sense in granting an existence income to the richest. Should the same sum be given to tramps and millionaires? Would it not be better to limit the granting of the citizenship income to those who do not earn more than a certain level? Alain Caillé, for example, has spoken out for an existence income on 'weak conditionality', which would be reserved for the poorest people.

Some also think that the elimination of a great number of social benefits for the advantage of the basic income is not acceptable, particularly because it would create a considerable transfer to the detriment of pensions (only those pensioners benefiting from resources other than their pension would have an income exceeding the poverty line). They are worried about seeing the emergence of a society divided into two classes of: on the one hand, those who would have only the citizenship income to live on, and the other those who would have a job in addition to it. 'The right to housing, for example', writes Michel Husson, 'would it be better guaranteed by the distribution of monetary allowances or by the socialisation of the offer of housing? ... Would it not be better to extend the field of public services and benefits to ensure the reality of social rights?'[259] Others also point out that it is quite contradictory to wish to restrain the productive sphere by means of a citizenship income when this income would be drawn from it.[260] This is joined by another objection: since the distribution of the citizenship income is ensured by the state, whose budget depends partly on the profits of businesses, if these profits fall, does not the income risk ceasing to be guaranteed? This is the argument advanced by Jean-Paul Lambert, according to whom 'eventually, such an income threatens its own system of financing'.[261]

---

259 *Contre Temps*, 18, February 2007.

260 Cf. Jean-Marie Harribey, 'Le cognitivisme, nouvelle société ou impasse théorique et politique?', *Actuel Marx*, September 2004.

261 Cf. *Prosper*, 18, 2007, p. 8.

The sociologist Guy Aznar esteems the idea 'pernicious', for, according to him, the citizenship income would place the individual in a situation of total social dependence. For him, as for Michel Husson, society should not rely on a right to income but on a sharing of work in the name of the principle 'work less to let everybody work'. Philippe Van Parijs and Yannick Vanderborght have replied to this argument by asserting that the citizenship income also constitutes a mode of work sharing.[262] Jean-Marie Harribey is also hostile to the citizenship income for the reason that work today remains an 'essential vector of social integration'. The right to work should thus continue to take precedence over the right to income, and the substitution of the concept of 'full-time work' for that of full-time employment represents only a 'liberal diversion'. 'Only work', thinks Harribey, 'is a creator of value capable of being distributed in the form of monetary incomes.'[263]

Finally, several authors fear that the establishment of a citizenship income may disarm all radical dissent. Not only would the guaranteed income favour the flexibility of work, but it would stabilise, reinforce, and perpetuate the system in place. Certain liberals, we have seen, are, in favour of an existence income which would take the form of a negative tax. Michel Husson thus thinks that 'it is futile to wish to subvert capitalism by opposing to it the claim to a guaranteed income if one leaves to it the mastery of commercial production'.[264] 'The allocation of an income', he adds, 'does not affect the fundamental social relations', for which reason he thinks it preferable to fight for the reduction of work time and for the creation of new gratuities.

That is clearly the fundamental question. It was indeed posed by André Gorz shortly before his death, in a text that appeared in June 2007 in the journal *Mouvements*: is the establishment of a guaranteed social income of

---

262 Philippe Van Partijs and Yannick Vanderborght, *L'allocation universelle* (Paris: La Découverte, 2005), p. 61.
263 Jean-Marie Harribey, 'Allocation universelle ou plein emploi?', *La Libre Belgique*, 22 June 2005.
264 *Critique communiste*, Summer–Autumn 2003.

a kind that would undermine the bases of capitalist society or, on the contrary, that would consolidate or save it? One could in fact maintain that, in the context of a progressive rarefaction of employment, capitalism will be able to survive only by a distribution of purchasing power that no longer corresponds to the value of work. The citizenship income would then be the means of continuing to favour the consumption of produced goods with a view to making a profit. Gorz himself replied, 'It is, in the claim to a guaranteed social income, not a matter of pursuing the illusory goal of a reorganisation of capitalism. ... It is, on the contrary, a matter of conceiving this claim as a way of confronting capitalism where it considers itself to be unassailable but becomes in reality most vulnerable: on the level of production.' In other words, it would be a matter of social income opening the way to an appropriation of work and production — by allowing one to free oneself from production elsewhere than *in* production. 'Self-production outside the market', adds Gorz, 'that is to say, the unification of the subject of production and the subject of consumption, alone offers an exit to escape this determination of the content of needs and of the mode of their satisfaction by capital.'

We see that the discussion remains open. But the question deserves to be posed.

Afterword: Confronting the Capitalist System

The text that follows is a preface to a collection of articles that appeared in the magazine Rébellion: Louis Alexandre and Jean Galié (eds.), *Rébellion: L'alternative socialiste révolutionnaire européenne* (Billère: Alexipharmique, 2009).

It would be a grave error to think that socialism (a term used for the first time in its modern sense by Pierre Leroux[265] in 1834) did not originally have as its aim a reaction against the abominable exploitation of the proletarian masses that the Industrial Revolution had thrown into the big cities and subjected to often inhumane working conditions. The first socialists of course denounced this exploitation, protested against their working conditions, and demanded the establishment of social justice. But in rising up against the bourgeois class, they also rose up against the system of values which was borne by the latter.

All traditional societies have held economic and market values (characteristic of the 'third function' in the Dumézilian sense of the term)[266] as

---

[265] Pierre Leroux (1797–1871) was a French philosopher and political economist. He co-founded *Le Globe*, which was the newspaper of the Saint-Simonian movement. He first coined the term in an essay entitled 'Individualism and Socialism'.—Ed.

[266] Georges Dumézil (1898–1986) was a French comparative philologist who investigated the commonalities and characteristics of the various civilizations that have made up the Indo-European tradition. He postulated that one of their fundamental characteristics that they all share is a tripartite social structure, which came to be known as the trifunctional hypothesis, consisting of the priesthood, the warriors, and the labourers and merchants (the latter being the third function).—Ed.

inferior or subordinate values for the reason that the economy above all should not become autonomous in relation to the social sphere, to global society. The economic was 'built in' ('embedded,' as Karl Polanyi[267] said) into the social, and the social obviously was not reduced to the economic. It is with the bourgeoisie, as a class bearing values that were characteristic of it, that the 'merit' lies of having established the economic sphere, at the same time that it asserted itself and precisely in order to assert itself, first as an autonomous and then as the dominant sphere. From this point of view, all European history can be read as a history of the rise of the bourgeoisie, in favour of whom the ideas that they bore were progressively established: individualism (against the significance of social relations), the cult of efficiency and utility (against the ethic of honour), and the normalisation of interest (against charity and gifting).

The bourgeoisie has historically driven itself like a wedge into the social structure, rejecting by the same stroke aristocratic values (which it forced itself at the same time to ape without understanding their basis, that is, honour and disinterestedness) and working class values (at the top of which was the 'common decency' evoked by George Orwell and of which we shall speak again). The rise of the bourgeoisie has put an end to everything that could remain of common goods in daily life, that is to say, of goods which were not yet subjected to individual appropriation, of spaces of life which could be the object of a common enjoyment. In England, for example, the 'enclosure' movement[268] converted open fields and common pasturelands into separate territories possessed individually by some people, which contributed to the encouragement of rivalries in the rural world and thus the social disintegration of communities. At the same time, the

---

267 Karl Polanyi (1886–1964) was a Hungarian-American economist and sociologist. His book, The Great Transformation, showed how what he termed the 'Market Society' arose through historical developments in England, gradually replacing the traditional communal approach to economics with the attitudes of liberalism.—Ed.

268 Prior to the thirteenth century, agricultural land was free for anyone to use. Following statues that were enacted at that time, such land became exclusively the property of its owner, known as enclosure. This often led to the eviction of peasants from their homes and the loss of their means of livelihood and led to a number of revolts, although the process of enacting enclosure throughout England never ceased.—Ed.

bourgeoisie set about monetising everything that had avoided being evaluated in this way in the past. This is what Karl Marx had already confirmed in a famous passage of *The Communist Manifesto*, which one cannot tire of citing: 'The bourgeoisie, wherever it has got the upper hand, has put an end to all feudal, patriarchal, idyllic relations. It has pitilessly torn asunder the motley feudal ties that bound man to his "natural superiors," and has left remaining no other nexus between man and man than naked self-interest, than callous "cash payment." It has drowned the most heavenly ecstasies of religious fervour, of chivalrous enthusiasm, of philistine sentimentalism, in the icy water of egotistical calculation. It has resolved personal worth into exchange value, and in place of the numberless indefeasible chartered freedoms, has set up that single, unconscionable freedom — Free Trade. In one word, for exploitation, veiled by religious and political illusions, it has substituted naked, shameless, direct, brutal exploitation.'[269]

In *Capital*, Marx also observed that 'at the base of the capitalist system, there is a radical separation of the producer and the means of production'. Capitalism in fact is deeply dividing, the capitalist mode of production resting on a double separation: the separation of the producers among themselves and their 'radical separation from the means of production'. This double separation creates and generalises the commercial relation between men on the one hand, society very soon no longer being imaginable except on the model of the market, and on the other hand, salaried work, the wage-earning system being the form of the exploitation of work which objectively forces the workers to submit themselves to the holders of capital and the owners of the means of production. Such a development is generally represented as resulting at the same time from the 'laws of history' (historical necessity in the historicist version of the ideology of progress) and from a 'nature' reconsidered from the angle of an ideology oblivious to what essentially constitutes it (the market is presented as the 'natural' form of social exchange, when it was in reality established at a relatively recent

---

[269] *The Communist Manifesto*, in Karl Marx, *Selected Writings* (Indianapolis: Hackett, 1994), p. 161.—Ed.

date, and economic harmony was supposed to result from the 'spontaneous' adjustment of supply and demand also being presented as 'natural' in bourgeois apologetics). Marx says further that this allows the ruling ideology to proclaim as 'everlasting truths, the trite ideas held by the self-complacent bourgeoisie with regard to their own world, to them the best of all possible worlds'.[270]

Liberalism is closed to all social perspective to the extent that, faithful to its intrinsic reductionism, it can analyse society only from the standpoint of the individual and understands it only as a sum of individuals and individual utilities. The notion of a common good, that is to say, a good whose enjoyment is situated prior to all possibility of sharing, is meaningless in its eyes. 'There is no such thing as society', said Margaret Thatcher![271] All that liberalism recognises is a diversity of egoistic and selfish aspirations whose free movement, it maintains, paradoxically ends — through the exercise of the 'invisible hand' — in the general harmony and 'happiness' of all and, at the same time, that this cannot be reconciled to a collective adherence to a shared idea of the good life. From the liberal point of view, there are only individual values, no collective values, and no collective project that can be legitimately structured on them. Liberalism never sees the collective character of individual difficulties and miseries, which it always tends to attribute to chance circumstances or individual psychology. As for politics, it is understood, from this perspective, only in the form of a procedural neutrality reduced to mere technical expertise and to 'rational' management administration, a process of neutralisation which is equivalent to ignoring and eliminating the very essence of politics. That is to say, that a good political decision always comes down to deciding among several possibilities in the name of values which are incarnated in the people.

---

270 *Capital*, vol. 1 (Mineola, New York: Dover Publications, 2012), p. 93.—Ed.

271 Thatcher said this in a 1987 interview with *Woman's Own* magazine. Thatcher went on to say, 'There is living tapestry of men and women and people and the beauty of that tapestry and the quality of our lives will depend upon how much each of us is prepared to take responsibility for ourselves and each of us prepared to turn round and help by our own efforts those who are unfortunate.'—Ed.

It is in reaction to this development that the magazine *Rébellion* has been forcefully proclaiming the necessity of a 'revolutionary socialist rupture' for some years. Faithful to the spirit of the immortal Commune of 1871,[272] its young team claims to follow the original form of socialism, which was directly opposed to the world of capital. In my opinion, nothing could be better. In each issue of *Rébellion* a brief programmatic statement appears ('Our Positions') which I wholeheartedly subscribe to — excepting, perhaps, the reference to 'National Bolshevism',[273] which seems to me to refer to a notion not only linked to obsolete historical circumstances but also contradictory in relation to the rest of the text (one cannot at the same time reject 'centralising nationalism' and claim to represent a 'state of a federalist type' while adhering to a National Bolshevism whose revolutionary spirit was based on an exacerbated Jacobin centralism). But it seems clear to me that *Rébellion* is also situated in the tradition of innumerable popular uprisings and peasant revolts, from the Peasants' War[274] to that of the Demoiselles,[275] of the English Levellers and Diggers,[276] of the Lyonnais

---

[272] The Paris Commune briefly took control of Paris between 18 March and 28 May 1871. It broke out due to increasing disaffection among the workers and the rise of socialist movements in the city, who seized the moment of chaos following France's defeat by Prussia to attempt to create self-government for the lower classes and overturn the established order. The Commune enacted many socialist, anarchistic, and progressive reforms during the brief period before it was violently put down. Ed.

[273] Several groups claim to be National Bolshevik, both in Russia and abroad. National Bolshevik ideology, which emerged after the First World War as an attempt to synthesise Communism and nationalism, was originally formulated by some participants in Germany's Conservative Revolution, such as Ernst Jünger and Ernst Niekisch. National Bolshevism was also present among some members of the anti-Soviet White movement and even among some Soviet Communists in the days of the Russian Civil War, although Lenin and Stalin both opposed it. Regardless, elements of the ideology re-emerged in Stalin's brand of nationalism, which began to appear in the 1930s. Several groups in present-day Russia have adopted the name.—Ed.

[274] The Peasants' War broke out in the German regions of Europe in 1524–25, in which the peasants fought to escape their serfdom and for the Protestant ideals that had been established by Luther. They were brutally defeated by the Holy Roman Emperor Charles V, and it is believed that more than 100,000 peasants were killed.—Ed.

[275] The War of the Demoiselles was fought between the peasants of the Ariège region of France and the state forest guards and local charcoal makers between 1829 and 1831, who were attempting to defend their right to use the forests in opposition to the restrictions that had been placed on them in the 1827 Forest Code. The local peasant men carried out their attacks while dressed as fairies. Attacks continued sporadically until the 1870s.—Ed.

[276] The Levellers were a movement during the English Civil War, in 1648–49, that favoured popular sovereignty. They were crushed by Cromwell. The Diggers were Protestant revolutionaries who were forerunners of anarchism and socialism in many ways. They established several communities in England in 1649, but were likewise suppressed by Cromwell's government.—Ed.

Canuts,[277] but also of the Vendée rebels[278] and the Chouans,[279] whose revolt against the 'infernal columns' of the bourgeois revolution of 1789 was very far from being reducible to a 'royalist and clerical' reaction. Rebellion, rupture, socialism, revolution: in a few words, everything has been said.

Everything has been said, but it is also there that the difficulties begin. For, a recourse to the inspiration of the original socialism — a recourse and not a return — cannot avoid a reflection on what has happened since then. Not only is it necessary, when one hears capitalism being attacked, not to limit oneself to the 'artistic critique' directed against 'bourgeois philistinism', which has often been the mark of romantic anti-capitalism, but it is also necessary to situate capitalism in a long-term context to understand what distinguishes nineteenth-century capitalism from present-day capitalism, the capitalism 'of the third type.'

In the first phase of the history of capital, the interests of the wage-earners were linked to the interests of their employers in a purely negative manner, as in a zero-sum game: the lower the salaries, the greater the employers' profits. The interests of the two classes were thus directly opposed to each other with evident clarity, since everything that was won by one was automatically lost by the other. But this first capitalism, which forced itself to reduce salaries as much as possible, of course risked seeing growth interrupted or slowed down by crises of overproduction. The holders of capital then realised that salaries, by determining purchasing power, also constituted the engine of consumption. They thus had to ensure a certain distribution of wealth, a redistribution certainly insufficient to limit the income gaps, but which could at least allow the absorption of an increasingly

---

[277] The Canuts were silk workers in the Lyon region of France in the nineteenth century, and were subject to extremely poor working conditions. They mounted revolts three times, in 1831, 1834, and 1848.—Ed.

[278] In 1793, during the Reign of Terror, the citizens of the Vendée region of coastal France, who were supportive of both the clergy and the monarchy, began an uprising against the revolutionary Republican government. Following the defeat of the uprising in February 1794, the Committee of Public Safety ordered the Republican forces to conduct a scorched-earth razing of the area and the mass execution of its residents, including non-combatants, women and children. Several hundred thousand people are estimated to have been killed out of a population of 800,000.—Ed.

[279] The Chouan uprisings took place in the western regions of France between 1794 and 1800.—Ed.

more important production by wage-earners henceforth regarded above all as consumers.

It is precisely this decisive change that the Fordist compromise incarnates, which was imposed when employers began to understand that there was another way to increase their profits: paying their wage-earners more in order that they could buy from them the goods that their labour force produced. Fordism marks the beginning of the advent of mass consumption, but also the major turning point towards reformism. As soon as the accumulation of profits came to be considered as profiting everybody globally, albeit at the end of a certain delay and in spite of persistent inequalities, of which the rise of the gross domestic product (GDP) and the expansion of the middle classes give evidence, the revolutionary perspectives receded. This is the phenomenon that Alfred Sauvy described with his theory of 'dumping': the accumulated profits at the summit of the social pyramid end up, at the end of a certain period of time, descending in part towards the base. From then on, it is only a matter of negotiating a better distribution of the 'fruits of growth'. The trade unions, one after the other, gave up fighting capitalism directly, and were concerned only with making their members benefit as much as possible from the profits that it yielded. This second phase of the history of capitalism, marked by the crisis of 1929, the Second World War, and the Cold War, is thus also the era of compromise. The only objective of the trade union organisations is to obtain an increase in real salaries in keeping with the productivity gains of labour. At the same time, the establishment of a social welfare state, Keynesian and socialist, allows the consumer-producers to obtain a minimum of security, at the risk of also becoming welfare dependants, at the same time as it accelerates the process of individualisation (due to the allocation of resources to the individual) and appears to contribute to the dissolution of classes.

In the Fordist phase, especially during the Thirty Glorious Years between 1945 and 1975, the economies still functioned with systems of financing that were radically different from those that we have known since the Thatcher-Reagan years, that is to say, the milieu of the 1980s. At that time, the development of capitalism yet remained relatively aligned to nations. This is no longer the case in the era of 'turbo-capitalism', which corresponds to the third wave in the history of capitalism, which is characterised by the rise and growing autonomisation of finance capitalism, and by the growing power of the holders of capital, and more particularly by the shareholders, who are today the veritable owners of the companies listed on the stock exchange.

The growing power of shareholders goes hand in hand with the ever-growing autonomisation of finance capital that Rudolf Hilferding[280] had already described at the beginning of the twentieth century, in reference to what Marx had written before him on 'fictional capital' (the pyramid of financial securities) and the 'administrators' of finance capital. This autonomisation creates a growing imbalance between real production and monetary phantasmagoria. Wishing to obtain a maximal return on their investments as rapidly as possible, the shareholders force the reduction of salaries and the opportunistic delocalisation of production towards emerging countries where the rise of productivity goes hand-in-hand with very low salarial costs. The result is that everywhere the increase of surplus value benefits capital gains rather than work incomes, salarial deflation in turn engendering the stagnation or the lowering of the purchasing power of the majority of people and the diminution of global solvent demand. At the same time, a number of functions that were earlier fulfilled by the welfare state are either transferred to international organisations or thrust upon personal psychology and entrusted to the 'life policy' of the individual himself.

---

280 Rudolf Hilferding (1877–1941) was an Austrian socialist and economist who was the chief theoretician of the Social Democratic Party of Germany during the Weimar Republic. In his 1910 work *Finance Capital*, he described how the pluralistic liberal capitalism that had previously dominated Europe had given way to monopoly finance capital, which he believed was the result of capitalists displacing the nobility in European society, and beginning to use state interventions to protect their own interests.—Ed.

What is called 'neoliberalism' today — generally to avoid having to speak of capitalism — is thus, in many respects, a restoration of the original capitalist system in its most brutally destructive elements, by placing workers in competition under the effect of international free-tradeism and the complete mobility of capitals, which creates an excess of pressure before which the trade unions, whose leeway continues to be primarily restricted within the national framework, are today almost impotent. Capitalism rediscovers its predatory character of the epoch of Thiers,[281] Guizot,[282] and Mac-Mahon.[283] Whereas, in the second phase, salaries contributed above all to the formation and development of domestic demand, in the third, they become considered again as merely a cost. The new element today is that delocalisations deregulation largely permit an escape from working class claims and trade union pressures: if the latter become too strong, businesses leave and establish themselves elsewhere where fiscal, ecological, and social standards are less restrictive. Job precariousness then becomes the rule. It is relatively contained, but also carefully maintained in order to impose fear of unemployment, to cause increasingly low wages to be accepted, and to disarm revolutionary demands. The consequences are well-known: a crisis of over-accumulation, growing inequalities in the distribution of incomes, crazy competitions between prices and salaries, and so on, while one witnesses a downward reorientation of the trajectory of profit rates, according to the diagnostic posed by Marx in the third volume of *Capital*, a reorientation accelerated by the growing substitution of human labour by mechanical labour in increasingly saturated markets, beginning with the market of real solvencies.

---

281 Adolphe Thiers (1797–1877) was the French head of state at the time of the Paris Commune of 1871, which he crushed.—Ed.

282 François Guizot (1787–1874) was a French politician who had sought, as Prime Minister, to suppress the demonstrations that led to the 1848 Revolution, and he later favoured restricting the vote to propertied men.—Ed.

283 Patrice de Mac-Mahon (1808–1893) was a French Marshal who led the troops who suppressed the Paris Commune.—Ed.

In this third phase, relative pauperisation is once again promoted, along with the promotion of inequalities, which the reformists limit themselves to making a 'moral' critique of, forgetting to say that they are also politically intolerable. Within every country, but also between countries, the rich are increasingly richer, and the poor increasingly poorer. Whereas in the era of the Thirty Glorious Years, when one entered the middle class one would not leave it again, this is no longer the case. The middle class does not stop becoming poorer and can only manage to maintain its standard of living by becoming indebted at the same time as its solvency diminishes. Speaking generally, enrichment no longer benefits the whole of society, but inflicts incalculable damages on it.

The present strategy of the capitalist system is thus to reduce salaries ever more and constantly aggravate the precariousness of the labour market, in this way bringing about a relative pauperisation of the working and the middle classes who, in the hope of maintaining their standard of living, have no other option but to go into debt.

What lessons can be drawn from this historical review, outlined here in large strokes? The first, in my view, is the confirmation that it is impossible to reduce the capitalist system to a simple economic form and to envisage the capitalist system only in its financial aspect. There is an anthropology of capitalism, a type of capitalist man, a capitalist imagination, a capitalist 'civilisation', a capitalist lifestyle and, as long as one has not broken with capitalism as a 'total social fact', and not challenged 'the entirety of the alienated lifestyles which are structurally linked to the capitalist imagination of limitless growth and consumption' (Jean-Claude Michéa), it will be futile to claim to be fighting capital.

The genius of Karl Marx, beyond all that one can disagree with in his thought, which is not unimportant, was to understand that the very notion of the accumulation of capital implied at once the globalisation of the market and also the commodification of all social activities, the transformation of everything into merchandise, the reduction of human relationships to simple relations of interest and utility, and the absolute rule of money. It is in this sense that he speaks, not without reason, of 'universal prostitution'. His superiority in relation to the other theoreticians of socialism is to have produced an analysis of capitalism which, going far beyond the merely economic approach, describes in detail the manner in which the reign of capital ends in commodity fetishism and the reification (*Verdinglichung*) of social relations, and to have posed as his objective, not only a more equitable redistribution of the alienating goods of market consumption, but a reappropriation of the 'ontological quality of our real human relations in the communal space of the social being, finally freed of all valuation'.[284]

Going beyond all moralising points of view to affirm the historicity of the categories according to which a society is led to consider itself, Marx, like Hegel before him, was able to recognise in the system of interests the endpoint of a long process of disenchantment with the world and with the very essence itself of bourgeois civil society, and in utilitarianism at once the typical intellectual form (ideology) and the social form of the epoch of bourgeois capitalism. Doubtless, his only error was not to have seen that the theory of utility is immanent in the economic sphere itself, including in the economic form that he himself advocated. In the same way that Nietzsche thought that he had opposed the philosophy of Plato, Marx wished to oppose the bourgeois theory of utility the ideology promoted by the bourgeois economic science of his time, without realising that his critique was still articulated from a deeply economic conception of the essence of man which, confusing the history of man with that of production, makes productive activity the very principle of the self-creation of humanity.

The irrationalism which is inherent in the capitalist system, as Claude Guillon notes, 'may be read in its inability to take into consideration whole sections of reality, such as the finitude of available geographical space, the exhaustible and degradable character of natural resources, the fragility of

---

[284] 'La domination capitaliste, le communisme, les communaux et lémancipation ontologique de l'être de l'homme', anonymous online text, 2008.

the ecosystem, etc.'.[285] But the capitalist system is also completely incapable of assessing the unrealism of its theory of value, its theory of competition, its belief in the 'invisible hand' which is supposed to be at work in self-regulatory and self-regulating markets, and its analysis of the 'irrationality' of politics and power. Capitalism, finally, nourishes a lack of culture, which it replaces with specialised technological knowledge — for the sole reason that it needs it. Only a ruling idea reduced to the slogans of the spectacle of the market allows the market to expand throughout the world. Only a symbolic imagination reduced to the narcissism of competing interests can justify the absolute rule of merchandise and allow the transformation of every individual into a merchant.

The engine of capitalism is not the production of goods and services, as is too often said, but the profit that this production allows, a profit that is maximised through the exploitation of work and the labour force. The notion of profit is based on itself: on the abstraction of exchange value, of which money is the support, whether material or (increasingly more often) immaterial. All modern egalitarianism is basically built on the monetary model, which is also by definition the sphere of profitability. One man and another man, one dollar and another dollar: the same. Whereas each of these is unique and irreplaceable, men are perceived as interchangeable in the way that money is defined as the universal equivalent, and as that which permits the reduction of everything to the equivalence of commodification and calculability, once its qualities are removed and reduced to quantities.

In *Grundrisse*, Marx very justly observes, 'But from the fact that capital posits every such limit as a barrier and hence gets ideally beyond it, it does not by any means follow that it has really overcome it, and, since every such barrier contradicts its character, its production moves in contradictions which are constantly overcome but just as constantly posited.'[286] It is the

---

285 Claude Guillon, '"L'économie réelle": une fiction capitaliste', online text, 19 November 2008.

286 In John E Elliot (ed.), *Marx and Engels on Economics, Politics, and Society* (Santa Monica, California: Goodyear Publishing Company, 1981), p. 114.—Ed.

rule of the *Ge-stell* evoked by Heidegger, the rule of this immense planetary misfortune that is represented by the general submission of the world to the market rationale, the reign of quantity, the rationale of profit, the axiomatic force of interest, and the transformation of all values into merchandise. An endless submission, in both senses of the term, to the extent even that the breaking out of the *Ge-stell* has to do above all with *hybris*, immoderation, lack of limitation.

To oppose internationalism to this immoderation, to this lack of limitation typical of the utilitarian system of the *Ge-stell*, is so much more ineffective in that capitalism is more than anything else 'a citizen of the world' (insofar as this expression has a meaning). The merchant has no other fatherland than the place which allows him to maximise his profits, as Adam Smith had already observed, and the tendency of capitalism to ignore borders dates from its origins. Borders constitute a limit, and thus an obstacle. They derive from the system of the Earth, whereas mercantile and commercial activity is by definition 'maritime':[287] it is developed in a world where no border can be traced, a world where only waves exist, fluxes and refluxes. If capital, as we have already said, remained for a time governed by the nation, today it has emancipated itself from every particular attachment. To the same extent that it is the bearer of unlimited aspiration, capitalism is not only deterritorialised by nature, but also constitutes the best means of abolishing territories as privileged places of social life.

Capitalism knows no other pluralism than the multitude of products, which is only an appearance of diversity. It aspires to a vast, homogeneous market where men would all aspire to the same possessions, and where the specificities of culture and mentality would never hinder the system of capital. It aspires to remodel minds through the sole desire to have, and through an obsession with merchandise. It considers as superfluous, transitory, or non-existent everything that cannot be reduced to numbers. In

---

287 The German jurist Carl Schmitt, taking a lesson from geopolitics, wrote, 'World history is the history of the wars waged by maritime powers against land or continental powers and by land powers against sea or maritime powers', in *Land and Sea* (Washington, DC: Plutarch Press, 1997).—Ed.

this way it causes all those areas which had formerly escaped commodification to be subjected to it, bit by bit. In this way it shows itself to be the producer of a one-dimensional man, a man with no internal or imaginary life other than that of merchandise, of a man without characteristics, with a mechanical body, and a formatted, conditioned mind aspiring to 'happiness' through having, and no longer experiencing any other passion than the burning desire to maximise his own interests. This is the 'last man' of whom Nietzsche spoke.

One can, from this point of view, only agree with the team of *Rébellion* when it defines the fatherland as 'a bodily link between workers, derived from their collective activity and strong solidarity in the face of the destructive globalisation of its traditional and cultural essence'. But this reminder should not make us forget that the 'fatherland' can also be used as a mystifying fiction when, under the cover of national unity, or of a 'sacred union',[288] this reference tends to cause the class struggle to be forgotten. We should clearly distinguish what the fatherland is for the people and what it is for the bourgeoisie, that is, a simple instrument for class warfare.

But one should also have the courage to question the ideology of work, that is to say, the value and the significance of work itself at a time when the latter is in the process of again becoming a central theme in social debate. It is not enough to denounce the alienation resulting from work; it is also necessary to unmask work itself in relation to what there is about it that is intrinsically alienating, which Marx rarely did. Many commentators have already emphasised the ambivalent character of work (Bourdieu spoke of its 'double truth'). The wage-earning system, which was imposed and standardised only after meeting with strong popular resistance, has no doubt 'liberated' or 'emancipated' some, but it has also alienated the majority. It remains today, as has often been said, a force for socialisation and a factor in identity: the unemployed person, 'useless to the world' (Robert

---

[288] The sacred union was a political truce that was called in France during the First World War, in which the Leftist parties agreed not to call any strikes or protests while the war was going on.—Ed.

Castel), is in a way disgraced in the eyes of his nation; he no longer has the means to integrate himself into the social body. But there is the other side of this coin, which cannot be reduced to the predatory manner in which the labour force continues to be exploited, be it by the soft violence of a 'business culture' which intends to abolish Taylorist workflows only to substitute new forms of domination in their place, and by the rise of a general climate of precariousness in jobs ('social insecurity').

One of the great mistakes of the ideology of progress has been to view the past retroactively, in terms of tendencies that were actualised in the nineteenth century in particular, under the reign of the triumphant bourgeoisie. From the condition of women in the nineteenth century, it was deduced that this condition should necessarily have been even worse prior to that time. From the exploitation of men by capital in the age of the Industrial Revolution, it was similarly deduced that this exploitation must have been even more frightening in preceding centuries. It seems to me that it was from this perspective that Karl Marx was able to praise the capitalist bourgeoisie in ambiguous terms for having abolished the feudal mode of production, and thereby guiding the development of the forces of production in the right direction. Contemporary historiography has taught us that things were less simple.

It is, in any case, precisely because capitalism is not only an economic system that a radical struggle conducted against it would betray itself by situating itself solely within the scope of quantity. Besides which, reformism has always consisted in reducing the struggle to the demand for a relative improvement in the conditions of exploitation by capital rather than in a demand for an abolition of capital. In 1865, Marx already stigmatised the social democrats who, by limiting themselves to claiming 'an equitable salary for a day of equitable work', did not take into consideration that they contributed in this way to the acceptance of the system that they otherwise criticised. To paraphrase Rosa Luxemburg,[289] they fought for a society where the slaves would simply be better fed. Such an attitude is not very different from that of those observers who assure us today that it is enough to 'regulate' or 'make ethical' the capitalist system in order to avoid its most negative effects.[290]

Marx said that in his view, Communism was not 'an *ideal* to which reality [will] have to adjust itself' but 'the real movement which abolishes the present state of things'.[291] Socialism certainly intends to put an end to the exploitation of man by man, but if it wishes to be faithful to its most fundamental aspiration, it must also aim at escaping from the dictatorship of credit and the impregnation of minds with market values. What it should seek to establish is not even 'equality', this term which has caused so much ink to flow and which can encompass very different things, but rather autonomy.[292] It is basically a matter of choosing between well-being or having more, of re-establishing the conditions of the social life that Marx called *Gemeinwesen*,[293] by redefining the conditions of the adjunction[294] of the 'I' and the 'we'.

We are far from that. Today we are experiencing the historic moment of globalisation, that is to say, of the global, international diffusion of the market ideology. The man that globalisation ordains is the man without

---

289 Rosa Luxemburg (1871–1919) was a German-Jewish Communist leader who was executed by the Freikorps for her role in the Spartacist uprising in January 1919, during the German Revolution.—Ed.

290 'Anti-capitalism does not offer any solution to the present crisis', proclaimed Nicolas Sarkozy, without laughing, on 25 September 2008, during a talk in which he also affirmed, very seriously, that 'the financial crisis ... is not the crisis of capitalism, but the crisis of a system that has distanced itself from the most fundamental values of capitalism, that has, in a way, betrayed the spirit of capitalism'!

291 *The German Ideology* (New York: Prometheus Books, 1976), p. 57.—Ed.

292 Jean-Claude Michéa remarks very correctly that 'the purely abstract equality of citizen monads always ends by increasing real inequalities and in this way reinforcing the domination of class' (*La double pensée: Retour sur la question libérale* [Paris: Flammarion-Champs, 2008]), p. 223).

293 Community.—Ed.

294 'Adjunction' is a term derived from field-theory referring to the relation between a field-extension and its subextensions.—Ed.

characteristics (Musil)²⁹⁵ and the one-dimensional man (Marcuse),²⁹⁶ at once a monad and a nomad, is thrown on the planetary market of non-life. Nature is devastated by man, who has installed himself as its 'sovereign master', as Descartes wanted it, but in doing so man has cut himself off from his foundations and henceforth becomes an artefact himself: human material. At the same time, liberal democracies have become oligarchies directed by a media- and politico-financial capitalist New Class, largely practising a social endogamy and for whom elections are only a necessary ritual, on the margins of which are exercised the true 'governance' of the nominated and the co-opted on the international level, the governance of experts and technologists protected from the overly volatile, distracting, and, finally, dangerous moods of voters who 'vote badly'. We thus witness, on the one hand, the neutralisation of politics, which is caught in the vice of economics (the market) and morality (the ideology of human rights) and, on the other, the increasing separation of politics and power, which is the major characteristic of late modernity. What remains are the eternal engines: power, sex, and money.

Social life thus finds itself plunged into insignificance and anomie.²⁹⁷ Cornelius Castoriadis spoke of an 'epoch of a rising tide'²⁹⁸ which is also that of integral privatisation, of the 'procedural republic', of generalised social disconnection, of mass narcissism, and the axiomatic nature of interest. One could also say: nihilism. Widespread economic ignominy based on

---

295 Robert Musil (1880–1942) was an Austrian novelist. In his principal work, *The Man Without Qualities*, the main character remains indifferent to the world and its values, allowing himself to be shaped by external circumstances rather than by any inner characteristics.—Ed.

296 Herbert Marcuse (1898–1979) was a German philosopher and sociologist associated with the Frankfurt School. In his primary work, *One Dimensional Man*, in which he claimed that the integration of individuals into the system of production as consumers in both capitalism and Communism was resulting in the rise of people with no capacity for critical thought or nonconformism.—Ed.

297 In sociology, anomie refers to a society that has ceased to provide ethical guidance to those of whom it is comprised.—Ed.

298 Cornelius Castoriadis (1922–1997) was a Greek-French philosopher who investigated the nature of society and the individual under capitalism and modernity. In his book, *The Rising Tide of Insignificancy (The Big Sleep)*, he claimed that the contemporary world is defined by a growing desert of nihilism and conformism in all spheres of life. The book has been translated in its entirety online at www.notbored.org/RTI.pdf.—Ed.

the monotheism of the market and the religion of endless growth, the envelopment of the consumer in the society of the spectacle,[299] the legitimation of the inauthentic, the impoverishment of the symbolic imagination, and mass delusion as a method of organising all the atomised individuals, all this ending in the colonisation of being by the imperialism of credit and appearances. This is in fact is quite precisely nihilism — total loss, absolute dereliction.

* * *

'No transformation comes without an anticipatory escort', said Heidegger.[300] Where, then, is the 'escort' today who is intellectually structured and resolved to act? Where is the means of once again producing a collective in a world that is prey to atomisation, where the citizens have become infantilised consumers? And finally, the eternal question with which we are now confronted more than ever before: where is the historical or socio-historical subject whose action will determine the significance of the times to come?

I do not think that the future is in the recourse to the 'multitude' of which Hardt and Negri are apologists, legitimising in this way a capitalism of the third type which does not stop producing these anonymous, deracinated, and interchangeable multitudes by destroying borders. I think that it can only be in the people. But how is it possible not to see that, today, this very word has become problematic?

The people of Paris did not survive the repression of the Commune of 1871. More generally, the French people have been bled white by the revolutionary wars and those of the Empire, and above all by the First World War, the great European civil war and the unmentionable slaughter which set the old continent ablaze and made it bleed. At the battle of

---

299 The 'society of the spectacle' is one of the principal ideas of the French Situationist thinker, Guy Debord. He saw the spectacle as one of the means by which the capitalist establishment maintains its authority in the modern world—namely, by reducing all genuine human experiences to representational images in the mass media, thus allowing the powers-that-be to determine how individuals experience reality.—Ed.

300 'Overcoming Metaphysics', in *The End of Philosophy* (Chicago: University of Chicago Press, 2003), p. 110.—Ed.

the Chemin des Dames, the offensive of General Nivelle alone resulted in 281,000 deaths, wounded, and missing in action in a little more than a month.[301] The First World War was many things, but it was first of all an opportunity for the European bourgeoisies to settle their accounts with the old working class and those peasant revolutionaries who had for so long incarnated the 'dangerous classes'. When the conflict ended, one counted eight million dead and twenty million mutilated in France. The workers' movement, which had not resisted the illusion of nationalism and a 'sacred union', the real aim of which was to resolve the crisis of overproduction and to raise the rate of capital gains, was effectively decapitated it for a long time. Capitalism hurried to reinstall itself, standing atop the mass graves.

Obviously, we should not overly idealise the people. It is not immune to envy and *ressentiment*.[302] In the history of the workers' movement, there there has been no lack of critiques of the bourgeoisie, but in reality all they were expressing was resentment stemming from not belonging to it and the secret desire to enter it. Nor have we been lacking theoreticians who saw in the people the proof of the 'natural goodness' of man, imagining that it is corrupted only from without, alienated by social structures whose arrival thus became incomprehensible. If social evil, the *fons et origo malorum*,[303] is 'society' while man is 'naturally good', how does one explain that this society has so many detestable characteristics? This is the old problem of theodicy. From the Christian point of view: how can a world created by an all-powerful and infinitely good God be inhabited by evil? From the 'progressive' point of view: how can societies composed of 'naturally good' individuals become so bad?

---

[301] Three battles were fought at the Chemin des Dames; Benoist is referring to the second, fought in April-May 1917, which was an attempt by the French to inflict a decisive defeat on the Germans, but instead resulted in a German victory.—Ed.

[302] *Ressentiment*, literally 'resentment', has a much stronger meaning in French. It suggests the endless repetition of the disgust that one feels towards a person or thing, resulting in a deep-seated aversion that becomes part of a person's essential nature.—Ed.

[303] Latin: 'the source and origin of our misfortunes'.—Ed.

Not to idealise the people means also not to be deceived regarding human nature. The idea that man is fundamentally good and that he is led astray only by a few wicked people — whose existence one cannot then explain — is one of the classical errors of a 'Left' that has imbibed the optimistic philosophy of the Enlightenment. Man is in reality neither naturally good nor naturally bad but, insofar as he is *Weltoffen* (open to the world) (Arnold Gehlen),[304] capable of the best as well as of the worst, capable of going beyond himself or of falling below himself, and capable of either conquering his autonomy or of vegetating in heteronomy. Evil is not always due to external circumstances, but can also result from the weakness, or desires, of man. To believe that the people cannot be deceived, that they are incapable of voluntarily doing evil, that it would be enough to remove their external obstacles to automatically cause it to find its 'own', or, further, that human nature is spontaneously oriented towards the common good (and economic harmony) in a way that the end of alienation would lead every individual to automatically begin acting in accordance with the interests of the many, is to fall into an angelism which can only end in disappointment. Jean-Claude Michéa, elsewhere so lucid, does not avoid this error when, after having evoked the 'moral values spontaneously shared by a great part of the working classes', he limits himself to stigmatising the 'will to power of some'. This implies that the majority, once left to itself, would be immunised against egoism and the desire for power or the will to do evil, the latter then appearing only as a 'perversion' and, in any case, as an exception.[305] Jacques Julliard sees very clearly when he writes, 'But to say that man is capable of

---

[304] Arnold Gehlen (1904–1976) was a German philosopher who was active in the Conservative Revolution.—Ed.

[305] We do not have the time to develop a critique on this point, but it seems to us that Michéa is totally mistaken when he affirms that liberalism considers it a 'pessimistic and desperate anthropology' (*La double pensée*, p. 87) because it is related to the tradition, Augustinian and Hobbesian in origin, of an intrinsically bad human nature. Liberalism certainly affirms that man naturally aims at satisfying his best interests, but, far from concluding from this the idea that he is a 'corrupt sinner', it is, on the contrary, to affirm that it is there a matter of an eminently positive trait, the addition of 'private vices' being supposed to end in a social optimum and the spontaneous adjustment of individual egoisms to produce finally the happiness of all (cf. Mandeville and Adam Smith). The philosophy of the Enlightenment, at once because it adheres to the theory of the *tabula rasa* and denies original sin, professes on the contrary a complete optimism regarding human nature.

evil does not mean that he is also capable of good. He must be treated as a free being, and not as a potential delinquent or as an angel from heaven.'[306]

However, even if all its members are not so to the same degree, the people remain no less the privileged depository of common decency, of that 'common decency' which George Orwell made the characteristic of ordinary people, of the 'people with little' (that is to say, of those who are much but who possess little): a sense of honour, loyalty, honesty, goodwill, generosity, propensity to mutual aid, confidence, a sense of the common good, and adherence to the rationale of giving and of returning benefactions. Michéa here is perfectly right in affirming that the market society manages to survive only by appealing to non-market values that it simultaneously tends to cause to disappear (this is one of its principal contradictions). Julliard also declares that liberal society survives 'only by continuing to draw freely on pre-liberal values common to Christian, aristocratic and proletarian societies'.[307] It is equally from this perspective that one should agree with Emmanuel Todd, according to whom 'the true drama for democracy does not reside so much in the opposition of the elite to the mass, as in the lucidity of the mass and the blindness of the elite'.[308]

In September–October 2008 (no. 32), the editorial in *Rébellion* was titled, 'Neither of the Left, nor of the Right: Revolutionary socialism!' Underscoring that the Right-Left cleavage 'is not for us an insurmountable framework for our political thought', for 'there are no values or ideas belonging in a proper and definitive way to the Right or to the Left', this text recalled the immense difference that exists between original socialism and the 'Left': 'The history of the Left begins in the tradition of the bourgeoisie called "progressive" which, profiting from the Dreyfus affair, was led to

---

[306] Jacques Julliard, *Le choix de Pascal: Entretiens avec Benoît Chantre* (Paris: Flammarion-Champs, 2008), p. 293. Julliard adds: 'My problem, that is, my political problem, is to reconcile an ideology of the Left with an anthropology of the Right. I believe strongly that the final aim of all society is to combat injustice; but I believe no less strongly that this combat is a combat not against external constraints alone but against human nature itself, such as it lives and prospers in each of us' (*Ibid.*, p. 304).

[307] *Ibid.*, p. 306.

[308] Emmanuel Todd, *Après la démocratie* (Paris: Gallimard, 2008), p. 223.

conclude a strategic alliance with the workers against the reactionary and conservative forces in order to preserve its gains.'

I of course approve this stance, but with one difference. The formula 'Neither Left nor Right' is in fact not new. It already has a history. This history reveals to us that, in the past, this expression was frequently used either as a means for legitimising a relationship, ambiguous to say the least, to the capitalist system — that is to say, in the final analysis, to mask the reality of the class struggle, or quite simply to mask an actual adherence to the Right (a contemporary political process). This is the reason why I prefer the formula 'neither Right nor Left', which gives rise to an inquiry into the point of view that one seeks to express, namely to the formula 'both Right and Left', which means basically the same thing, but which puts the emphasis on the spirit of dialectical synthesis and of *Aufhebung*[309] that is the characteristic of intersecting systems and of new cleavages.

From the Right, apart from individual developments, there is obviously nothing to expect. If today it has not moved entirely to the side of money, at least it does not stop maintaining a scarcely artistic blurriness around the omnipresent reality of capital. In this way, the customary reluctance it feels with regard to society is added to a complete incomprehension of the historical period in which we live. Except in some small circles, the Right has abandoned what in the past could have constituted its legitimacy: its fidelity to the ethic of honour, charity, and disinterestedness. The Right has come to possess and thereby it has been dispossessed. It has stopped reading Sorel[310] and Proudhon.[311] It prefers the predators of the CAC

---

[309] In Hegel's conception, *Aufhebung* means simultaneously to change and to preserve something, which he saw as being crucial to the dialectical process when two concepts interact with one another.—Ed.

[310] Georges Sorel (1847–1922) was a French philosopher who began as a Marxist and later developed Revolutionary Syndicalism. He advocated the use of myth and organised violence in revolutionary movements. He was influential upon both the Communist and Fascist movements.—Ed.

[311] Pierre-Joseph Proudhon (1809–1865) was a French politician and philosopher who opposed capitalism and did not believe in state ownership of property, instead believing that property should belong to workers' groups.—Ed.

40 to Bernanos[312] and Péguy.[313] Instinctively allergic to 'Marxism' and to 'Communism', it advocates the collaboration of classes — without ever having seriously read Marx (or Rousseau). The Right has become liberal, forgetting that it is the liberalism of the Enlightenment which began to bring about its defeat. On its margins it survives with its obsolete slogans, its outmoded nostalgias, and its fetishistic references. Restorationist ('it was better before'), it invokes the past like an alibi and makes history a refuge and a consolation. Always hostile to 'men in too large numbers', it lapses into racism and xenophobia, and also into Islamophobia in the name of an improbable 'clash of civilisations' (which plays the classic role of a diversion in relation to class conflicts). It has become blind and deaf to what is happening before its own eyes. It exhausts itself in sterile agitations, perpetually committing the same errors and caricaturing itself.

But the Left does not conduct itself any better. Historically, it has always been afflicted with four great defects: political universalism, quite different from concrete internationalism; the absence of a realistic anthropology (this is the error regarding human nature of which we have spoken); the belief in 'progress' (which causes many of the traits of society which have historically limited the influence of capital to be considered as 'archaic'); and a constant moralism (a secularised Christianity) tending toward a fixation upon complaints and grievances on principle and the exaltation of weakness. To this is added, still under the influence of the philosophy of the Enlightenment, the inability to analyse modernity as a progressive rise of the bourgeois values which engendered capitalism, whence the paradox that it persists, as Péguy defined it, in extolling 'as modern' the same world that it denounces 'as bourgeois and capitalist', without seeing that modernity constitutes above all the socio-historical context which liberal capitalism needed in order to form and develop itself completely.

---

312 Georges Bernanos (1888–1948) was a French writer who was anti-democratic in his beliefs.—Ed.

313 Charles Péguy (1873–1914) was a French writer who was both a nationalist and a socialist. He was killed in battle during the first days of the First World War.—Ed.

The Communist Party, which by the 1950s had succeeded in creating a truly popular political culture, and even a truly 'counter-society', by being at the same time the most nationalist and most internationalist of all the French political parties, has become a phantom (it garnered 1.9% of the votes cast in the presidential election of 2007). Social democratic and no longer Communist, it has progressively aligned itself with all the fashions and all the derivatives to which it should have been opposed. The Socialist party itself has become a liberal socialist party, the party of people who have not stopped integrating themselves into the upper middle classes by distancing themselves as much as possible from the people, a party of notables and officials relatively protected from the damage wrought by neoliberal capitalism and of the tumults of the global market (the officials do not risk being the victims of delocalisation). Its development can be symbolically summarised by the appointment of two of its members, Dominique Strauss-Kahn and Pascal Lamy, to the head of the two large, liberal international institutions that are the International Monetary Fund (IMF) and the World Trade Organization (WTO). With their increasingly nebulous vision of society, their apparatuses increasingly cut off from the working classes, and their vocabulary secretly divested — not only of the 'dictatorship of the proletariat' and of 'revolution', but also of the notions of 'struggle', of 'workers', 'labourers', of 'class enemy', and even of the opposition between capital and labour — the PS[314] and the PC[315] are also today instruments of the collaboration of classes. As for the history of the workers' movement, apart from some circles which make it the object of their study, it has been quite entirely forgotten. Among the young members of the PS

---

314 Parti Socialiste (Socialist Party).—Ed.
315 Parti Communiste (Communist Party).—Ed.

and the PC, who has ever heard of Émile Pouget,[316] Benoît Malon,[317] and Fernand Pelloutier?[318]

Under the pretext of 'realism', of 'adapting to modernity', and of recognising 'complexity', the parties of the Left do not stop running after the Right by appealing to 'social dialogue' and limiting themselves to calling for a 'spiritual supplement' to the dominant ideology. Incapable of learning from their successive defeats, they aspire to a better distribution of 'growth' just like the others, repeating, each more loudly than the other, the *mantras* of 'competition' and 'competitiveness'. Dumb in the face of the obscenity of advertising, having become a paradigm of all the social jargons, communing in the adoration of 'human rights', and forgetting the radical critique that Karl Marx made of it, the parties of the Left have led the workers' movement down the road of consumer consent. Their only objective is henceforth to 'make capitalism ethical', which comes down to leaving politics to return to a moralism evoking the epoch of the patron ladies[319] and social Christianity. The fashion of becoming a caricature of humanitarianism, of the charity business, and of 'care', is part of the same movement, which tends to replace social justice with the orchestration of compassions towards those who have been victimised in life (who are no longer workers or proletarians, but 'the most impoverished', 'the most neglected', the 'excluded', etc.), in this way forbidding themselves to analyse the system that is in place in a radically critical manner. Their claims are increasingly more fragmented, instead of aiming to unite against the common enemy. In a general climate of individualism in which commitments are increasingly more selective, ephemeral, and transitory, it is the very idea of a collective project that disappears.

---

316 Émile Pouget (1860–1931) was a French anarco-communist who was Vice Secretary of the General Confederation of Labour from 1901 to 1908.—Ed.

317 Benoît Malon (1841–1893) was a French socialist writer who served on the Council of the Paris Commune.—Ed.

318 Fernand Pelloutier (1867–1901) was a French anarchist.—Ed.

319 A 'dame patronesse' is a lady who undertakes social work in a Christian parish.—Ed.

'Conversion to economic liberalism, acceptance of financialised capitalism, cynical careerism of its high officials: the betrayal by the Socialist party of the values of the Left is evident', writes Emmanuel Todd.[320] The remark is correct, even if it would doubtless have been better to speak of a betrayal of socialist values, since the term 'Left' is so ambiguous. This assessment, in any case, has been repeated innumerable times. As Jean-Claude Michéa writes, 'reading the programmes of the Left and the extreme Left, one derives the curious impression from them that a socialist society (when perchance this "archaic" term is still employed) is fundamentally nothing more than the quiet continuation of the present lifestyle, tempered on the one hand by a more equitable distribution of the "fruits of growth" and on the other by a perpetual exhortation to fight against "all forms of discrimination and exclusion", whether the latter, besides, are real or purely fantastic.'[321] Whereas the Right has renounced the nation and the critique of money, the Left renounces socialism and every radical critique of the influence of capital. Both, in doing so, cut themselves off in like manner from the people.

This rallying of the Left to the market society, with its habitual correlatives (returns, calculability, competitiveness, profitability, etc.), has two aspects. On the one hand, it legitimises itself with the idea that, according to experience, the capitalist system is ultimately the one that has shown itself to be the 'most efficient' at producing goods and services in large quantities, which comes down to making efficiency in this field the essential criterion for judgement, without consideration of the price with which this efficiency is paid or the impoverishment that it introduces in other fields, without reflecting on the significance and value of what it is that is produced. The error here is in seeing in the capitalist system as only one economic form among others — in relation to which the others have shown themselves to be less functional — and interpreting its success as being the result of an in-

---

320 *Ibid.*, p. 27.
321 *Op. cit.*, p. 97.

evitable development. In this perspective it is is not very distant from social Darwinism. There follows from it an inevitability of reformism, since the capitalist system is viewed as the only possible one, or at least as the least bad one. When this is believed to be the case, what remains is to try to manage it. The other aspect is that this type of rallying is as good as an alignment to the ideal of unlimited growth at any cost and of indefinite material growth, which is precisely that of the capitalist system itself.

In the political vacuum left by the PS and the PC, a new radicalism 'of the Left' seeks to install itself, but it is rarely worth more than the reformists to whom it pretends to be opposed. Instead of defending the people, the extreme Left instead orients itself towards marginal struggles: toward providing aid to illegal and undocumented immigrants, to homosexual marriage (including egalitarian neofeminism), the extension of the right to abortion, the legalisation of soft drugs, the denunciation of sexual harassment, the support of 'suburban revolts' (the 'difficult quarters')[322] or the defence of 'contemporary art', all causes that the people do not give a damn about and to which they are even sometimes allergic. In doing this, it situates itself in the lineage of a May '68 of which one will remember only too well that, alongside a truly anti-establishment aspect (the critique of the society of the spectacle, a rejection of market values, the desire to serve the people, the biggest workers' strike in the history of France, etc.), it included a purely infantile, hedonist, and permissive, and thus deeply liberal, component which overwhelmed it. Those who wished forty years ago 'to play without restrictions' were not slow in understanding that it is liberal capitalism and the market society which would best permit them to realise this ideal. They said, 'Under the pavement, the beach'; they got Paris-Plage.[323] This extreme Left thus joins a social-democratic or 'bobo'[324] Left, hence-

---

[322] Difficult quarters are those quarters of Paris with high crime rates. In Paris, the suburbs are where the majority of the immigrant population lives.—Ed.

[323] This is a reference to the Paris-Plage scheme, which is an initiative to create temporary artificial beaches in Paris in the summer along the River Seine. It was initiated in 2002 by the Socialist mayor, Bertrand Delanoë.—Ed.

[324] Bourgeois bohemian.—Ed.

forth as liberal in terms of lifestyle as on the economic level, and for which the 'problems of society', the 'societal' and 'citizenship' questions, are visibly more important than political principles and demands.

Jean-Claude Michéa's great merit is to have shown the confluence between the different forms of liberalism, and the incoherence of the attitude that consists in affirming that one is liberal on the 'societal' level but not on the economic level. The two finally join each other. Economic liberalism and politico-cultural liberalism, writes Michéa, constitute 'the two parallel versions and (what is more important) complementary of the same intellectual and historic rationale', which explains why the majority of the pseudo-libertarian advocates of liberalism in lifestyle 'ended up by seeing the natural complement to the ideological axioms they began with in the market economy'.[325] The heirs of May '68 wanted to make people believe that the 'liberation of lifestyle' was the principal gain achieved by the movement, and even today they refuse to understand that this 'liberation', far from opposing the bourgeois world, was in reality perfectly in accord with the very spirit of liberalism, and corresponded very precisely to what one could describe as 'merely the supreme stage of the imperialism of credit and that which is false, and the next stage in the colonisation of sex by the free, fetishistic circulation of commerce and emptiness'. They thought they had undermined the established order by increasing 'transgressions' of all sorts, without seeing that these transgressions which fascinate them only left the field free for the system of consumption. Likewise, they failed to see that their challenges to the 'moral order' opened the way for the idea they claimed to oppose, and that this had allowed the people to free themselves from tradition only to be more tightly subjected to the dictates of advertising and fashion. It is not surprising that today they defend the cause of these 'youth of the suburbs' whose only regret — and the real reason for their anger, when they become vandals and burn their neighbours' cars — is

---

[325] *Op. cit.*, p. 14.

not to have been able to benefit as fast and as massively as they would have liked from the objects of market production.

In search of a substitute for the proletariat, the extreme Left has chosen as its aim the discovery of a historic subject which is emphatically not the people. It is difficult here not to evoke the problem of immigration. Like the unemployment situation of yesterday, immigration in fact represents primarily an industrial reserve army of capital which is exercising a downward pressure on salaries while simultaneously increasing profits. Simultaneously, the 'anti-racist' doctrine forbids any criticism of the population replacements which capital is bringing about in order to extinguish the revolutionary traditions of the European peoples, and by exiling the indigenous proletariat from its own history.

There is no doubt that contemporary 'anti-racism', which was formulated in the 1980s by organisations like SOS-Racisme,[326] was formulated above all to replace anti-capitalism and hide the Left's abandonment of its old ideals. The danger henceforth was 'Le Pen' and no longer capital. Better still, by combating Le Pen, they played into the hands of a capitalism too happy to find a new source of cheap labour in immigration that was malleable, open to exploitation, and completely ignorant of the revolutionary traditions of the French proletariat. All that obviously did not have anything to do with the necessary fight against racism. Those who today devote themselves to the unconditional defence of illegal immigrants and the 'undocumented immigrants' actually are continuing to 'offer to the capitalist class the cheap, submissive reserve army of which the latter has need as it attempts to free itself of the old European workers' disputes'.[327] The Besancenots and other Leftists, experts at incantatory neopopulism, and who only speak in the name of the people to make it keep quiet, constitute nothing today but the Left wing of the political apparatus of capital.

---

326 A French anti-racist organisation founded in 1984.—Ed.

327 Anonymous online text, 2008 (cf. Note 1).

Michéa has also shown very well how, in today's extreme Left, the formerly central figure of the proletariat and the exploited worker has been abandoned to be replaced by that of the 'excluded', of whom the homeless and the undocumented immigrants 'constitute at present the privileged media incarnation'.[328] This new category, with remarkably vague contours, allows one to avoid an in-depth analysis of contemporary alienation. The 'excluded' is also very often the immigrant or the 'young offspring of immigration', who is made a messianic figure by the rhetoric of the moment. This relegates those who are of local origin to their natural worthlessness, and the exaltation of whom, in a systematically lachrymose and compassionate and no longer insurrectionary and demanding, manner, serves above all to legitimise the 'deterritorialisation' (the generalised displacing) and the deconstruction of the principle of rooted national cultures in accordance with the liberal phobia of specific rootednesses, local habits, shared values, and inherited associations (along with the organic solidarities that they engender). This serves to accelerate a total universal mobility, causing individuals to be viewed as fundamentally interchangeable in a 'world without borders', which the capitalist system has made one of the primary conditions for participating in the market.

The historic subject which the Left identifies with is basically little different from this *lumpenproletariat* to which Karl Marx, who saw in it the dregs of urban society ('these dregs of corrupt individuals from all the classes, who have their base in the big cities'), denied all historicity, noting that its parasitism is reproduced, in 'luxurious' forms, by the social organisation of the ruling financial class 'by causing the available wealth of others to disappear'. 'The finance aristocracy', he wrote, 'in its mode of acquisition as well as in its pleasures, is nothing but the *rebirth of the lumpenproletariat on the heights of bourgeois society*.'[329]

---

328 *Op.cit.*, p. 54.

329 Karl Marx, *The Class Struggles in France: From the February Revolution to the Paris Commune* (Chippendale, Australia: Resistance Books, 2003), p. 38.—Ed.

But has the proletariat really disappeared? From the rise of individualism on the one hand and the expansion of the middle class on the other, it has been too quickly concluded that classes have disappeared and, therefore, the class struggle. The internal collapse and disintegration of the Soviet system has simultaneously spread the idea that liberal capitalism has triumphed over all its competitors, and that henceforth there are no more competitors to this system. They announced without laughing the 'end of ideologies' (when we are swimming in the ideology of merchandise) and the 'end of history' (when it does not stop returning). However, the damages of capital are always there, and they do not stop increasing. And it is again the distribution of socio-professional categories which, after the disintegration of the traditional political families, today remains the factor that allows one to best understand and analyse the electoral results. How does one in fact explain the rise of the Front National in the 1980s, the 'no' to the referendum of 2005,[330] or the exhaustion of the classical political parties without taking into consideration the milieus of the working class?

History has certainly not evolved, contrarily to what Marx believed, towards a direct confrontation between a homogeneous bourgeoisie and a proletarian mass. On the contrary, the reign of the upper middle class is characterised by dinners at Le Fouquet's and golden parachutes, while delocalisations, coyly travestied as the 'internationalisation of production', everywhere bring about layoffs and reductions in salaries. Social differences have not stopped increasing. If the peasants are on the way to extinction (agriculturists constitute no more than 1.6% of households), one counts today 20% workers and 11.5% wage-earners in France, or in total 50.8% of the working population. Besides, the tendency is towards the loss of status of the middle classes, more especially of the lower middle classes. Who can

---

330 On 29 May, France held a referendum on the treaty that proposed the establishment of a Constitution for the European Union. 55% of voters rejected the proposal.—Ed.

say that this counts for nothing?[331] It is among the workers that the plan for a European constitutional treaty was rejected most clearly in 2005 (81%), whereas in the 2007 presidential election, 82% of the heads of business voted for Nicolas Sarkozy. In March 2006, the workers favoured protectionism by 63%, for they know well that it is one of the conditions which must come to pass for salaries to rise once again.

The share of salaries in the GDP fell by 9.3% between 1983 and 2006, or a total of 120 to 170 billion euros which came every year to be added to the capital gains. Whereas the businesses of the CAC 40 registered record profits, the net salarial income did not significantly increase for 25 years (it even declined between 2000 and 2005). Those who possess capital thus control the lives of those whose work allows them to make their profits.

The disconnection of the political class from the people has also simultaneously brought about an oligarchic drift of the ruling class, the financial bourgeoisie, and with it the dictatorship of 'governmance' and the advent of a surveillance state and, at its base, the flourishing of 'populisms'. Democracy is now no longer the political form which causes the legitimisation of power to rest in the sovereignty of the people and which, because of this, is so much more faithful to its intrinsic inspiration that it allows for a greater participation of the citizens in public affairs. Liberal representative democracies not only no longer represent anything, but have become mere apparatuses in the hands of the New Class. The people are no longer represented, and that is the reason why it increasingly turns away from political life. The working classes do not recognise themselves in those who claim to speak in their name, and for whom 'populism' has become a derogatory term. One is oriented to a 'post-democracy' which is, quite simply, a democracy without a people. One no longer votes in it to choose the best, but only in the hope of eliminating the most harmful. And, as they end up revealing themselves in action to be one worse than the other, one no longer votes at

---

331 Cf. François Ruffin, *La guerre des classes* (Paris: Fayard, 2008); Marcel Gauchet, 'Les mauvaises surprises d'une oubliée: la lutte des classes', *Le Débat*, May–August 1990, text reprinted in *La démocratie contre elle-même* (Paris: Gallimard-Tel, 2002), pp. 207–228.

all. The spectacle, in its twofold aspect as advertising and 'entertainment', is one of the preferred instruments for the neutralisation of the suffrage. But it is not for nothing that, at the end of the nineteenth century, revolutionary syndicalists had already designated universal suffrage as a mystification that bore with it the myth of inter-class conflict and of 'social pacification'.

It is not the working classes that have disappeared, but the clear consciousness of its condition and of that which unites its members against a common enemy. This effacement of class consciousness ('class in itself', instead of 'class for itself') is not new. We know the works that have been published on 'false consciousness'.[332] There has never been a lack of authors who affirm that the misfortunes of the ruled derive first of all from the lack of awareness of their domination, or their irresistible tendency to be complacent in their chains and to seek their reinforcement: they are dominated because they do not know that they are so. Still, one should not abuse this interpretation, which one cannot however deny contains part of the truth. There is always some pretension in declaring that one knows, better than the people themselves, the real situation in which they find themselves and the feelings that they should experience. Many self-proclaimed vanguards have fallen into this trap, as well as theoreticians like Pierre Bourdieu, as has been emphasised several times by Jacques Rancière (who declares today that he has broken with Marxism precisely due to his rejection of the presupposition according to which men are dominated because they are unaware of their domination, in such a way that it would suffice to communicate to them the required 'knowledge' in order to allow them to liberate themselves). Subjection is not only explained by ignorance, even if false consciousness, such as is maintained today by the media for example, constitutes an incontestable cause of alienation. It can also be explained in terms of resignation, which leads one to live in a state of fatalism, by a lack of imagination, and by the forgetting of references that go hand-in-hand

---

332 False consciousness is what Marxists term the methods by which capitalist society deludes the proletariat. Engels regarded ideology as one of these things, as he wrote in a letter to Franz Mehring on 14 July 1893.—Ed.

with a lack of culture in general, and also by the doubt of the majority regarding their capacity to change things. But it is no less true, as Jean-Claude Michéa says, that it is difficult 'to describe or explain [the] new developments of liberal civilisation without resorting, in one way or another, to the philosophical concepts of false consciousness and alienation',[333] concepts which he notes in passing have, remarkably, disappeared from the vocabulary of the present-day Left.

It remains to the working classes, today simple aggregates of relatively heterogeneous social elements, to create what Antonio Gramsci[334] called 'collective wills'. That is the only means of returning to the people their dignity as political subjects suited to fulfilling their historic role. The term 'autonomy' may summarise this objective, as long as it does not make it synonymous with the ideal of the monad, that is to say, with the 'independence' of the atomised individual. Autonomy, for an individual as for a collectivity, is to act and to think for oneself — to become a post-Oedipal adult — and to conquer the means to decide for oneself the conditions of one's existence as much as is possible. There is no autonomy without a dialogical relationship, without a relation to the other. Autonomy, finally, cannot be attained through mere juridical independence or emancipation through a right to consume (which does not necessarily make demand solvent).

Michéa again says very correctly that, if one wishes to see the ordinary people to one day engagein a big, new collective project of autonomy and emancipation, capable of leading to a society where one will never again be able to live off the work of others, this movement 'will never start from the top'.[335] As André Gorz has also shown very well, it is in fact clear that it is necessary today to start locally, that is to say, from the places where life

---

333 *Op. cit.*, p. 35.

334 Antonio Gramsci (1891–1937) was an Italian Communist who was imprisoned by the Fascists. Unlike Marx, however, Gramsci did not see class as the subject of history, but rather 'collective wills', which are social groupings centred around a particular class. Gramsci felt that class struggle was an insufficient principle on its own, since there are also struggles taking place between collective wills within each class that must be viewed as part of the dynamic.—Ed.

335 *Ibid.*, pp. 174–175.

takes place: the district, the business, the municipal democracy. When a global change is impossible, it is first of all necessary to recreate spaces of freedom and social life which are, as it were, 'territories' removed as much as possible from the ruling controls, at the same time remedying social disconnection, causing shared values to reappear and initiating the beginning of a renaissance of active citizenship in the public sphere, linked to a more participatory and more direct democracy. This alone is capable of allowing the people to decide regarding that which concerns them for themselves, according to the principle of subsidiarity.

Those who are employed in this task can only be revolutionaries. The word should be used without grandiloquence. To be a revolutionary is not to delude oneself, in a romantic or nostalgic manner, with memories of barricades and armed insurrection, but to maintain in oneself a mental disposition which is totally alien to that which triumphs today in the world of the inauthentic and of alienation, and which is experienced as such. The revolutionary acts in a world from which he wishes to be totally estranged because he finds it abject, but which he nevertheless understands perfectly. That was already the advice that Georges Sorel gave to revolutionary syndicalist militants when he advised them to take the early Christians as their example: those who absolutely rejected the world that they were fighting against. The necessary attitude is that of the most complete critical radicalism. Critical radicalism — which is not synonymous with extremism, but much rather its opposite — certainly fights for the maintenance of peoples and cultures, but also for the preservation of what is human (and specifically human) in humanity, knowing that men only belong to humanity only in an intermediary manner. That is to say, they belong to it through the intermediary of the peoples and cultures that they have inherited, and whose eternal historical narrative it is their duty to extend as much as they can.

Rébellion has deliberately committed itself to this difficult path. It is sad to have to say that, at first, it is probably not its natural enemies, the masters of capital, who will show it the most hostility. The young team who run it will first have to confront the problems, the polemics, and the inevitable disappointments which are connected to the history of all organisations. Finally, and above all, it will have to confront those who are stupid, that is to say, those for whom its desire to draw new divisions can only be 'suspect'. The rulers have always applied the same motto: divide and rule. We must help those who have not understood that, when faced with a common enemy, everything else is secondary, to realise this plan. This is why the designation of the principal enemy is important.

The principal enemy is at once the most harmful and, above all, the most powerful. Today it is capitalism and the market society on the economic level, liberalism on the political level, individualism on the philosophical level, the bourgeoisie on the social level, and the United States on the geopolitical level. The principal enemy occupies the centre of the system. All those who combat the power of the centre along the periphery should support one another. But they do not. Some think instead that the most important thing is to know 'from where one comes' or 'from where one speaks'. It is they who, when a house is burning, ask those who come to put out the fire for their identification papers. In no case, in their eyes, can the enemies of their enemies be their friends. I think exactly the opposite. The enemies of my enemies are not necessarily my friends, but they are necessarily allies. I am notoriously not a Castroist, but I will always support Castro in his fight against American imperialism. I am notoriously not a Christian, but I will always support the Christians every time they struggle against the power of money. Those who reason otherwise do not have a sense of the priorities or the stakes. They are quite simply accomplices.

Rébellion is a small group. I do not know if this group will grow larger. I hope so. In any case, it has the merit of going to the heart of the matter. It is the bearer of a compelling hope and also of a will. It is a spark (*iskra*).[336] It is still too early to say if this spark will set the prairie on fire, as good

---

[336] *Iskra* means spark in Russian. It was the name of a newspaper published by Russian socialist émigrés in Europe during the first years of the twentieth century, and was initially run by Lenin.—Ed.

Chairman Mao said.[337] For the moment, it is not forbidden to blow on the embers to make the flame burn more strongly.

---

[337] In 1930 Mao published an article entitled 'A Single Spark Can Start a Prairie Fire'.—Ed.

Index

A

Agrarian Justice (Paine) 126
Allais, Maurice 38–51, 81, 106
Après la démocratie (Todd) 46, 169
Aquinas, Thomas 57
Aristotle 8–9, 57
Auber, Olivier 130–132
Aventis 89
Aznar, Guy 147

B

Balssa, François-Laurent 117–118
Bank of France 69–77
Basel III 73
Baudrillard, Jean 17
Baverez, Nicolas 23
Bergson, Henri 24
Bernanos, Georges 171
Besancenot, Olivier 45, 122
Bettencourt, Lilian 90
Bookchin, Murray 138
Bourdieu, Pierre 162, 181
Bouygues, Francis 116
Braudel, Fernand 11
Bresson, Yoland 125–144
Bretton Woods 26–28, 47, 102

C

CAC 40 88–89, 111–116, 170–180
Caillé, Alain 129–146
Calvin, Jean 58
Camus, Léon 69
Capital (Marx) 9, 151–157
Castel, Robert 100–110, 139, 163
Castoriadis, Cornelius 165
Castro, Fidel 184
Cato 57
Céline, Louis-Ferdinand 56
Centre de recherche pour l'étude et l'observation 96
Charlier, Joseph 127
Chauvel, Louis 99–100

Chemin des Dames 167
Chevènement, Jean-Pierre 33, 46
China 17, 30–39, 51–53, 67–68
Cohen-Tanugi, Laurent 46
Colombani, Jean-Marie 54
Connally, John 28
Cook, Richard C 142
Cordonnier, Laurent 92
Council of Nicaea 57

D

de Basquiat, Marc 144
Descartes, René 165
Dessertine, Philippe 75–76
d'Estaing, Valéry Giscard 69
De subventione pauperum (Vives) 126
Douglas, C H 128, 145
Duboin, Jacques 127–145
Duboin, Marie-Louise 127–145
Dumézil, Georges 149
Dupont-Aignan, Nicolas 82–84
Dutrieux, Janpier 126

E

El Karoui, Hakim 46–52
Empire (Hardt & Negri) 122–123
England 27, 42, 61–63, 150–153
European Central Bank (ECB) 63–77, 113
European Commission 53, 65–70, 118
European Economic Community 28, 66
European Financial Stability Facility (EFSF) 69–73
European Union 36, 51–53, 69–84, 144, 179
Ezekiel, Mordecai 37

F

Federal Reserve 26–34, 63–68, 113
Ferry, Jean-Marc 125–131
First World War 62, 153–171
Fitch Ratings 68
Ford, Henry 90, 108
Fourier, Charles 127

Fourtou, Jean-René 89
France 32–179
French Institute of Public Opinion 71
French Revolution 58, 126
Friedman, Milton 130
Front National 71, 179

G
Galbraith, John Kenneth 129
Genoa Conference 27
Germany 61–82, 153–156
Gesell, Silvio 127, 145
Glass-Steagall Act 77
Gold Exchange Standard 27
Goldman Sachs 65–73
Goldsmith, Jimmy 81
Gorz, André 131–148, 182
Gourévitch, Jean-Paul 121
Goux, Jean-Joseph 9
Gramsci, Antonio 182
Great Depression 11
Gréau, Jean-Luc 46–59, 71–76, 107
Greece 42, 61–82, 126
Group of Ten 28
G20 21–44
Guardian, The 80
Guigou, Jacques 123
Guillon, Claude 159–160
Guilloteau, Laurent 129
Guitton, Henri 131

H
Hardt, Michael 122–123, 166
Harribey, Jean-Marie 146–147
Hegel, Georg 140, 159–170
Heidegger, Martin 18, 161–166
Hewlett-Packard 89
Hilferding, Rudolf 156
Hirsch, Martin 137
Hoover, Herbert 47, 131
Hurd, Mark 89
Husson, Édouard 26, 107, 146–147
Husson, Michel 26, 107, 146–147

I
Imbert, Claude 54
INSEE 91–93, 143
International Monetary Fund (IMF) 21–33, 53, 70–74, 172
Italy 33, 61–75, 112

J
Jamaica Accords 28
Japan 28–33, 50, 63, 118
Jorion, Paul 65
Julliard, Jacques 22, 168–169

K
Keynes, John Maynard 48–59

Klein, Naomi 70
Kohl, Helmut 80
Kondratiev, Nikolai 11
Kousselas, Dmitri 72
Kudrin, Alexei 33
Kurz, Robert 123

L
Lafargue, Paul 139
Lafay, Gérard 84
Lambert, Jean-Paul 146
Lamy, Pascal 172
Landais, Camille 92
Laulan, Yves-Marie 14
Laws, The (Plato) 41–51, 79, 125–126, 151
Le Pen, Jean-Marie 177
Leroux, Pierre 149
L'illusion économique (Todd) 46
Lisbon Treaty 69
List, Friedrich 49, 75, 87
Lordon, Frédéric 13, 59, 76–78
L'Ordre nouveau 128
Luxemburg, Rosa 164

M
Maastricht Treaty 69, 81, 105
Mansholt, Sicco 129
Mao 185
Marc, Alexandre 48, 125–131, 144
Marcuse, Herbert 165
Marseille, Jacques 144–145
Marx, Karl 9–18, 139–182
Maurin, Éric 94
MEDEF 89, 117–122
Medvedev, Dmitri 33
Mercosur 36
Michéa, Jean-Claude 158–182
Miller, Henry 87
Mitterrand, François 80
Moody's 68–72
More, Thomas 7–185
Moulier-Boutang, Yann 129–135
Multitude (Hardt & Negri) 122, 129, 135
Murray, Charles 130–138
Musil, Robert 165

N
NAFTA 36–40
National Bank of Paris (BNP) 72, 88
Negri, Antonio 122–123, 166
Nemo, Philippe 89, 119
New Deal 19, 77, 137
Nietzsche, Friedrich 159–162
Nivelle, Robert 167
Nixon, Richard 17–27

O
Obama, Barack 20, 67

Organisation for Economic Co-operation and Development (OECD) 66–75
Orwell, George 90, 150, 169
Owen-Jones, Lindsay 89

P

Paine, Thomas 126–127
Palma, Norman 26
Parisot, Laurence 122
Parrot, Jean-Pierre 129
Passet, René 131, 145
Péguy, Charles 171
Peugny, Camille 99
Piketty, Thomas 88–92
Pinçon, Michel 94–95, 107–115
Pinçon-Charlot, Monique 94–95, 107–115
Plato 125–126, 159
Polanyi, Karl 150
Pompidou, Georges 116
Portugal 61–82
Pound, Ezra 32, 56
Proudhon, Pierre-Joseph 129, 170
Putin, Vladimir 67

R

Raffarin, Jean-Pierre 139
Rancière, Jacques 181
Raufer, Xavier 66
Reagan, Ronald 22, 64, 104, 156
Rébellion 149–169, 183–184
Restos du Coeur 95
Rhys-Williams, Juliet 130
Ricardo, David 38–46, 78
Rodrigues, Gustave 128–129
Roosevelt, Franklin D 27–48, 77
Rosanvallon, Pierre 112
Roubini, Nouriel 83
Russell, Bertrand 129
Russia 17, 30–33, 153

S

Sapir, Jacques 37–54, 84–85, 114–115
Samuelson, Paul 46, 129
Sarkozy, Guillaume 43, 93–95, 107–115, 139, 164, 180
Sarkozy, Nicolas 43, 93–95, 107–115, 139, 164, 180
Sarrazin, Jacques 127
Sauvy, Alfred 108, 155
SBF 120 89
Schäffler, Frank 74
Schlarmann, Josef 74
Schumpeter, Joseph 11
Second World War 13–36, 59, 117, 155
Séguin, Philippe 81
Smithsonian Agreement 28
Smoot-Hawley Tariff Act 47–48
Société d'économie politique 36
Solution du problème social (Charlier) 127

Sorel, Georges 129, 170, 183
Soros, George 17–18, 34, 87
Spain 42, 63–82
Standard & Poor's 68
Strauss-Kahn, Dominique 172
Sweden 28, 80, 109

T

Taiwan 33, 68
Tepper, David 87
Thatcher, Margaret 22, 64, 104, 152–156
Tinbergen, Jan 129
Tobin, James 129
Todd, Emmanuel 42–55, 169–174
Treaty of Amsterdam 53
Treaty of Rome 53, 66
Tribalat, Michèle 118–119

U

Union des industries textiles 43
United Kingdom 4, 80
United Nations 37, 91
United States 11–100, 113, 130–142, 184
Utopia (More) 126, 134

V

Valois, Georges 129
Vanderborght, Yannick 147
Van Parijs, Philippe 131–147
Vendée rebels 154
Vietnam War 27
Vinci 89
Vivant-Europe 144
Vives, Joan Lluís 126

W

Wajnsztejn, Jacques 123
Wallerstein, Immanuel 20–21
Weber, Max 7
Weiland, Jean 127
Weisbrot, Mark 80
Weiss, Raoul 78
Winock, Michel 10
Wintrebert, Raphaël 52–53
World Bank 31, 53
World Trade Organization (WTO) 36–64, 172
World War, First, see First World War
World War, Second, see Second World War

X

Xiaochuan, Zhou 31
Xiaonian, Xu 26

Z

Zacharias, Antoine 89
Zemmour, Éric 118
Zin, Jean 133–142

Other Books Published by Arktos

The Dharma Manifesto
by Sri Dharma Pravartaka Acharya

Beyond Human Rights
by Alain de Benoist

Carl Schmitt Today
by Alain de Benoist

Manifesto for a European Renaissance
by Alain de Benoist & Charles Champetier

The Problem of Democracy
by Alain de Benoist

Germany's Third Empire
by Arthur Moeller van den Bruck

The Arctic Home in the Vedas
by Bal Gangadhar Tilak

Revolution from Above
by Kerry Bolton

Eurasian Mission
by Alexander Dugin

The Fourth Political Theory
by Alexander Dugin

Putin vs Putin
by Alexander Dugin

Fascism Viewed from the Right
by Julius Evola

Metaphysics of War
by Julius Evola

Notes on the Third Reich
by Julius Evola

The Path of Cinnabar
by Julius Evola

Archeofuturism
by Guillaume Faye

Convergence of Catastrophes
by Guillaume Faye

Sex and Deviance
by Guillaume Faye

Why We Fight
by Guillaume Faye

Suprahumanism
by Daniel S. Forrest

The WASP Question
by Andrew Fraser

We are Generation Identity
by Génération Identitaire

War and Democracy
by Paul Gottfried

The New Reaction
by Rachel Haywire

The Saga of the Aryan Race
by Porus Homi Havewala

Hiding in Broad Daylight
by Lars Holger Holm

The Owls of Afrasiab
by Lars Holger Holm

Homo Maximus
by Lars Holger Holm

De Naturae Natura
by Alexander Jacob

Fighting for the Essence
by Pierre Krebs

Can Life Prevail?
by Pentti Linkola

The Conservative
by H. P. Lovecraft

The NRA and the Media
by Brian Anse Patrick

Rise of the Anti-Media
by Brian Anse Patrick

The Ten Commandments of Propaganda
by Brian Anse Patrick

Zombology
by Brian Anse Patrick

Morning Crafts
by Tito Perdue

A Handbook of Traditional Living
by Raido

The Agni and the Ecstasy
by Steven J. Rosen

The Jedi in the Lotus
by Steven J. Rosen

Barbarians
by Richard Rudgley

Wildest Dreams
by Richard Rudgley

Essential Substances
by Richard Rudgley

It Cannot Be Stormed
by Ernst von Salomon

Tradition & Revolution
by Troy Southgate

Against Democracy and Equality
by Tomislav Sunic

Defining Terrorism
by Abir Taha

Nietzsche's Coming God
by Abir Taha

Verses of Light
by Abir Taha

A Europe of Nations
by Markus Willinger

Generation Identity
by Markus Willinger

The Initiate: Journal of Traditional Studies
by David J. Wingfield (ed.)

Printed in August 2021
by Rotomail Italia S.p.A., Vignate (MI) - Italy